Praise for

I *Forgave* YOU *Yesterday*

"This book will free you with its common-sense approach for how to embrace the Atonement and let go of anxiety and depression. The solid principles of *I Forgave You Yesterday* will free you to live more abundantly today. It will resonate with anyone who seeks truth and is interested in positive solutions to real-life problems."

—Dr. Taylor Hartman, psychologist and author of *The People Code* and *The Character Code*

"We all know that the roads of life have many twists and turns, and it can be hard to navigate them. Many of us struggle to know how to tackle these obstacles AND apply the Atonement of Jesus Christ. As a counselor and a loving church leader, James has found a way to put these together. This is real practical help! *I Forgave You Yesterday* offers powerful hope and simple steps to more fully live the gospel of Jesus Christ *while* facing serious challenges. If you want help and hope to respond better to life's rough roads and do so with greater power in your faith, you need to read this book!"

—Jim R. Jacobs, LCSW, author of *Driving Lessons for Life: Thoughts on Navigating Your Road to Personal Growth*

"I've known and appreciated James's unique insight for over twenty years. He gets people and human nature, and he gets what Jesus wants for us. James uses his unique insight and the stories of everyday people to illuminate a simple path to peace and fulfillment."

—Mark Hopkins, author, entrepreneur, and founder of Crescendo Capital

"It has been a great pleasure to know James Skeen for many years. He has taken examples from his own life and stories from his practice to guide his readers in examining what it means to become whole. Life is messy and James uses real life examples to guide his readers to deduce their dependence on destructive tension relieving behaviors and to live in the now. His discussion of the difference between shame and guilt was practical and enlightening. I was envious of his wisdom when he shared with his client regarding interacting with the critical judgements his client was voicing internally that 'you were not created to serve the voice; the voice was created to serve you.' The Creator's design for us is to grow and thrive. James's insights will assist those struggling with their lives to find the life our loving God intends for them."

—Dr. Skip Barber, psychologist and professor

I *Forgave* YOU *Yesterday*

I *Forgave* YOU *Yesterday*

Receiving Christ's Atonement Daily

JAMES SKEEN

CFI
An imprint of Cedar Fort, Inc.
Springville, Utah

ISBN 13: 978-1-4621-2296-7

Published by CFI, an imprint of Cedar Fort, Inc.
2373 W. 700 S., Springville, UT 84663
Distributed by Cedar Fort, Inc., www.cedarfort.com

LIBRARY OF CONGRESS CATALOGING-IN-PUBLICATION DATA

Names: Skeen, James T., 1964- author.
Title: I forgave you yesterday : receiving Christ's atonement daily / James T. Skeen.
Description: Springville, Utah : CFI, an imprint of Cedar Fort, Inc., [2018] | Includes bibliographical references.
Identifiers: LCCN 2018028759 (print) | LCCN 2018034104 (ebook) | ISBN 9781462129447 (epub, pdf, mobi) | ISBN 9781462122967 (perfect bound : alk. paper)
Subjects: LCSH: Atonement--Church of Jesus Christ of Latter-day Saints. | Atonement--Mormon Church. | Forgiveness.
Classification: LCC BX8643.A85 (ebook) | LCC BX8643.A85 S54 2018 (print) | DDC 232/.3--dc23
LC record available at https://lccn.loc.gov/2018028759

Cover design by Wes Wheeler
Cover design © 2018 Cedar Fort, Inc.
Edited by Justin Greer and Emily Chambers
Typeset by Kaitlin Barwick

Printed in the United States of America

10 9 8 7 6 5 4 3 2 1

Printed on acid-free paper

Writing a book is not an easy thing. There are multiple moments of second guessing, frustration, and mental exhaustion. I am deeply grateful to friends, family and my Father in Heaven who have encouraged and contributed to this book, and I am especially appreciative to Laura E. Hilton for her contributions. She was able to refine concepts and help structure my writing in ways that had eluded me. I know that without her help, this book may never have become a reality.

Contents

Introduction

The Pool of Bethesda

Waiting at the Bishop's Office

I must have walked past the bishop's office at least ten times that night. To my fifteen-year-old brain, it felt more like one hundred, but I kept walking by even though Mutual had been done for a while. Trying to look nonchalant, I walked toward the lobby one more time to see if the bishop's door was open, just like I had the week before and the week before that. It hadn't been open any of those other weeks, but tonight might be different. Palms sweating, stomach aching, and head hanging low, I slinked one more time through the church building.

The door was open.

"James? Is that you? Come on in." The warmth of my bishop's voice struck me, as did his smile.

I hesitated. It didn't matter that I knew I needed to go in there. It didn't matter that I knew he would most likely help me. All that mattered was that I had messed up. I had made a mistake I knew I shouldn't have. I knew I was going to let him down when I told him. I was so disappointed in myself, and I knew God was disappointed in me too. I should have been better, stronger, wiser. I was a member of Christ's church. I attended church on Sundays. I was a Boy Scout. I had knowledge, and I knew that should make me better than the average sinner.

But I wasn't.

And that hurt. A lot.

We've all had moments like this. Whether we're outside the bishop's office, hearts heavy with sin, or simply lying in bed at night, knowing that God knows our weaknesses but being too afraid to talk to Him about them—we've all been there.

And it hurts. A lot.

Sometimes the pain of those moments is mental, and we feel like our thoughts are hamsters on never-ending wheels trying to escape reality. Sometimes the pain is physical too. Our stomachs hurt from the nerves, our mouths feel dry, our faces feel hot. There is almost always emotional pain in those moments, and it fills our hearts with heaviness and despair.

The deepest pain, however, is often spiritual. Our wounded spirits are limping along, and no matter how we try to brace them up, we cannot deny the fact that our past weaknesses, regrets, and sins are dragging us down and don't bode well for our futures. Guilt and anxiety flow in like the tide, and we know that our very souls are at risk of being lost in a sea of spiritual anguish.

That kind of pain isn't easy to live with. Elder David A. Bednar said, "Guilt is to our spirit what pain is to our body—a warning of danger and protection from additional damage."[1] It is the pain of a guilty conscience, that warning sign of additional damage, that propels us to the bishop's office, to our loved ones, and to our knees seeking healing.

Waiting at the Pool of Bethesda

There are many stories in the scriptures of healing, but there is one that, to me, is different from the rest. It is the story of a man seeking relief in a deep way but who, through the process of healing, finds not only relief but something greater. He finds wholeness. That story is the one of the man at the pool of Bethesda.

You probably remember the story. It starts with a man, crippled and alone—the Apostle John tells us—who has suffered for thirty-eight years with what scripture simply calls "an infirmity" (John 5:5). We don't know the exact nature of the infirmity, but we know it was serious because not only did it last thirty-eight years but also the man was surrounded by "a great multitude of impotent folk, of blind, halt, withered" (John 5:3). He was gathered with people like him, those in serious pain who were seeking relief in the best way they knew how. For the man at Bethesda, his pain had defined a great deal of his past, and without healing, he had no future.

The solution he found was a particularly miraculous one at a particularly miraculous pool. The pool of Bethesda had five porches and was probably used for ritual washings by the Jews of Jesus's time. Literally named, "house of mercy," the pool at Bethesda was also said to be home to miracles. The scriptural account tells us that "an angel went down at a certain season into the pool, and troubled the water: whosoever then first after the troubling of the water stepped in was made whole of whatsoever disease he had" (John 5:4). The man was waiting faithfully by the pool for the angel so he could be healed. If he could just make it in those waters fast enough, he knew that the past pain of his life could be erased, and his future would be brighter.

There was only one problem though. The man wasn't fast enough on his own to make it to the water before the angel's power ran out. There was no way for him to get in and be healed without someone else's help. And, unfortunately, he was surrounded by people who were not at all capable of helping him. They were in the exact same predicament he was. Hurt and suffering, they were all waiting and hoping for a miracle to change their lives.

Modern Pools of Bethesda

Spiritually many of us are like this man, waiting at our own modern pools of Bethesda. We find ourselves having suffered from pain of some sort or another for a long time. It could be pain from a wayward child or pain from a difficult marriage. Maybe you're divorced or had a difficult childhood, perhaps even suffering abuse or neglect. Perhaps you are burdened by sin, sin you've tried to repent of but you still don't feel clean. You go to church. You read your scriptures. You pray. You fulfill your calling. You do everything a faith-filled Latter-day Saint is supposed to do.

But somehow or other, you are falling short. You're still in spiritual pain.

Spiritual pain often leads people down a couple of well-worn mental paths: one of regret and shame for the past and the other one of anxiety and worry for the future. For most of us, they end up being the only trails through mortality. But just because they are common doesn't make them the paths we were meant to follow. Heavenly Father has a different path, one that is not filled with regret, shame, anxiety, or worry. In fact, it is so different from the paths we are used to following that many of us don't always believe another path exists. But God does have a different path, one that was in place from the beginning, and it is the only path He means for us to follow.

You've probably found yourself on the paths of regret and shame and anxiety more than once. Think about how much time you spend worrying about your past pain and regrets and planning how to have a pain-free future. You say to yourself, "If I can just pray harder, then my son will come back to the Church." Or you might say, "If I can just make more money now, I'll be free of financial burdens later." "If I'm more righteous, the Spirit will touch my husband's heart and our marriage will be saved." But no matter how diligently you walk the paths of sadness and worry, things never get better. Some moments you feel lifted, sure, but by and large, the nagging feeling that things could fall apart any minute is always lurking in the background.

That's certainly where I was—a fifteen-year-old boy standing outside my bishop's office. My spirit was hurting, and my head was about to explode from the fear of actually talking about my sins. The fear of my past mistakes and the worry about what was awaiting in my future were weighing me down, but the pain I was feeling at that moment seemed worse than any I might feel in the future. I needed healing, I wanted the pain to end, so I risked going into the office.

The True Nature of Healing

Healing was different from what I expected it to be. My bishop and I talked. I told him what I needed to tell him, and he guided me through a repentance process. There was so much relief that night. I walked out of his office feeling lighter and more hopeful than I had in weeks. I started to understand what the Savior meant when He said, "Come unto me, all ye that labour and are heavy laden, and I will give you rest . . . for my yoke is easy, and my burden is light" (Matthew 11:28–30). I had come unto Christ by confessing my sins, and I actually felt better, lighter.

Unfortunately, that feeling didn't last forever. My initial relief from confessing my sins and weaknesses was only a small part of the healing I needed. I had repented of my sins, but I was still haunted by the memory of what had happened, and I was worried about how I would handle similar situations in the future. As time passed and I made other mistakes and discovered more of my own weaknesses and flaws, my heart was still hurting, and my head still felt like it was going to explode. After all, didn't it say somewhere in the scriptures that God would forget our sins but if we screwed up again He'd remember them all?

I needed something more than just the relief of confession and repentance. I needed to become someone different. And no matter how hard I tried, that was proving to be difficult. My efforts alone weren't enough to get the job done. Even though I had come unto Christ through my confession and repentance, there was still more I needed to do to be truly healed.

But I had no idea what that was.

A Grander Solution

The man at the pool of Bethesda found himself in a similar situation. Before waiting at Bethesda, he had probably tried any number of things to find relief from his pain. Finally, after thirty-eight years, he hit on the miracle of Bethesda and thought that one spiritual event would give him the healing he needed.

It was then that the man met Jesus Christ. The scriptural account tells us, "When Jesus saw him lie, and knew that he had been now a long time in that case, he saith unto him, Wilt thou be made whole?" (John 5:6). The man, not knowing who Jesus was or what He really had to offer, responded, "Sir, I have no man, when the water is troubled, to put me into the pool: but while I am coming, another steppeth down before me" (John 5:7). He thought that Christ was offering to help him complete his own limited plan for pain relief, but Christ had more to give.

Can you imagine the man at Bethesda and his surprise at Christ's response? Rather than talking to him about how to get in the pool or just walking away, the Savior responded with a very simple command. I imagine that Christ slowly looked over the man, taking in every part of his condition, then looked him in the eyes and said the words that wouldn't just give the man relief but would also change his life in the most profound way: "Rise, take up thy bed, and walk" (John 5:8).

How often do we look to Christ only to see our plans instead of His? How often do we try to tell Him what to do simply because we don't really understand who He is?

Just like I needed more than a simplistic confession and repentance episode to really heal my soul, the man at the pool of Bethesda needed more than a dip in the water to be whole.

He needed to change his situation entirely. He needed the Son of God to change what had already happened to him and what was going to happen to him in the future. He needed Christ to help him change his very soul. He needed an atonement.

Christ, through His infinite Atonement, offers each of us the same deal, to rise and walk away completely healed. His Atonement means that we can experience more than just pain relief from the spiritual wounds of life. We can be completely healed and made whole from our pains at their root cause so that we don't have to deal with the fear and spiritual damage. But to do this we have to do more than seek a onetime dramatic event of repentance.

Each of us, with our sins and regrets and anxieties, is waiting at our own figurative pool of Bethesda. We come initially seeking that pain relief. We want the pain of our past sins and regrets wiped away. We want to know that our futures will be less painful than our pasts because Jesus Christ will fix us. But Christ wants to do more than that for us. He doesn't just want to relieve our pain (although He definitely does do that and is always willing to do so). He wants us not only to feel better, but also to rise, take up our beds, and walk with Him to a newness of life (Romans 6:4).

Christ asks us: Are we simply seeking pain relief, or do we want to be truly healed? Do we want to be made whole?

Finding Wholeness

"Wilt thou be made whole?" is one of Christ's most heart-piercing questions. It is both straightforward and enigmatic. Of course all of us want to be made whole, but what does that mean?

This is a question I often ask myself as I examine my life. My pondering has led me to realize that this question has far-reaching implications. Not only does it ask us about what we want right now but it also begs other questions. Who do we really want to be? What are we willing to do to get there? What are we willing to change to get there?

There have been times in my life when I sought out the Lord for just His pain relief, not understanding the offer or the process to become whole. I defined joy as the absence of pain, and righteousness as the absence of sin. I wasn't particularly interested in wholeness. I wanted pain relief. I wanted comfort and happiness and to not have to work so hard. Perhaps in my deeper-thinking moments I thought of repentance as making me more complete, as having a whole life—one with lots of different experiences that made me wise.

But none of my definitions ever came close to glory of our Savior's. Christ defines *wholeness* as so much more. He tells us it is an abundance of life. "I am come that they might have life, and that they might have it more abundantly" (Romans 6:4). Wholeness for Him means abundance. Not to have just enough but to have more than enough. Wholeness through Him means He can heal us, cleanse us, give us hope, and actually fill in the emptiness that so often plagues us during our mortal lives. He mends the spiritual micro-fractures that come from living as fallen people in a fallen world. Through Him we can see ourselves as more than the sum of our near misses and forgiven sins. He allows us to both love our potential selves of the future and forgive the mistaken self of the past—and most important, to be at peace with our flawed actual self of the present moment.

Do you see the difference between the abundant Atonement that Christ is offering us and the repentance-only version so many of us use? Without even realizing it, we have put a limit on God's grace, letting it extend to repentance only and not our daily lives. This is a smaller version of Christ's love, and it is not what He means for us to have.

Think about it this way: when we fully access Christ's Atonement, we not only feel relief from the pain of our past regrets and sins and our worries about the future, but we also feel happiness on an eternal scale in the present. We don't just want relief from our fears and sadness so we can avoid further pain; we want to be completed by Christ so we can feel supernal peace and joy today, every moment, right now.

We can do more than just wait at the edge of the gospel and hope for pain relief. We can be made whole.

What Is This Book About?

My goal with this book is to help you find a clearer connection to the Savior Jesus Christ. I want you to feel His love and healing every moment of your life. I want you to feel like a whole person in both body and spirit. I've spent hundreds of hours teaching and thousands of hours counseling individuals as a bishop and a therapist, trying to help them start to feel that power from Him. This book is the culmination of my efforts and observations.

As you read, you'll follow the stories of three different people. Their stories are conglomerates of the people I have worked with over the years and the problems they have sought to overcome. Their stories are 100 percent true in that sense. Their problems, attitudes, and even the conversations are ones that have occurred in my office as a counselor and a bishop and will probably occur again. I've included them so you can start to see how to apply the principles presented in the following chapters.

After all, many of the principles of *I Forgave You Yesterday* are easy to say but take fortitude to apply. I want you to get a feel for the ups and downs that happen when you set out on the true path that God means for you to follow. Some days you will do better. Other days you won't. But the speed of this process doesn't matter so much as the orientation of your life: new patterns, more godly patterns, and an eye single to His glory.

The first section of this book, chapters one through four, lays out the problems that most of us face and how they separate us from God—and it isn't necessarily for the reasons you think. It isn't just sin that distances us from our Father in Heaven. You have to understand the true nature of the problem before you can understand the solution, so we are going to spend some time getting to the roots of our spiritual disconnects.

The second section, chapters five through eight, details the most effective practices I've found to help individuals change the way they think. It's important to master your thoughts and beliefs because your thoughts and beliefs shape your desires and actions. If you don't change your beliefs—your actions—no matter how hard you try and how much willpower you have, you will revert to what you were doing before.

The third section, chapters nine through twelve, are the action chapters. They are the chapters that show you how to change your behaviors to make room for the abundance that Christ's Atonement offers. Just how faith without works is dead, it isn't enough to just change how you think. You've got to go and do. These actions are both specific and open ended. This means they are meant to not only point in the right direction but also to let you shape the way you move in that direction.

The final section, the conclusion, is actually like more of a gate. This book is about leaving Bethesda and entering the gate that will take you beyond the limits of your pain and into, hopefully, a new, more dynamic partnership with Christ where you can feel His atoning power in dynamic ways in your life.

In the Doctrine and Covenants, the Lord promises His people, "I will go before your face. I will be on your right hand and on your left, and my spirit shall be in your hearts, and mine angels round about you, to bear you up" (Doctrine and Covenants 84:88). That is the power of the Atonement. The attitudes and practices in this book are meant to help you feel and see that power that is being sent your way, so that you too can—one day at a time—follow Christ and find lasting healing.

Note

1. David A. Bednar, "We Believe in Being Chaste," *Ensign*, May 2013, 44.

Part One

Wilt Thou Be Made Whole?

And a certain man was there, which had an infirmity thirty and eight years.

When Jesus saw him lie, and knew that he had been now a long time in that case, he saith unto him, Wilt thou be made whole?

The impotent man answered him, Sir, I have no man, when the water is troubled, to put me into the pool: but while I am coming, another steppeth down before me.

—John 5:5–7

There are many in the Church today who wait, metaphorically speaking, by the pool of Bethesda hoping to be carried into the healing waters. War veterans might suffer from horrific memories and broken bodies. Other Saints might suffer from the isolation of depression or addiction. Widows live alone or face failing health; families feel devastated by a child's illness or an unexpected accident; and caregivers work long, lonely hours taking care of a family member. Who will carry these infirm to the pool?

—Anne M. Tanner

("Carrying Others to the Pool of Bethesda," *Ensign*, January 2011, 63.)

Chapter 1

The Atonement and Who We're Meant to Be

Carolyn was a busy Mormon mom. She was a dedicated wife and mother of four who somehow managed to balance it all while working full time from home and serving in the Relief Society presidency in her ward. She was one of those women other women looked at and often said, "How does she do it?"

Carolyn couldn't answer that question if anyone had asked her—not that they did. She was too busy. She had always been classified as an over-achiever: valedictorian of her high school, getting her bachelor's and master's degrees in four years, and always working while taking care of her kids and her home. As an oldest child born into the Church with a father who served as a bishop more than once, Carolyn knew there were commandments to be kept and an example to be set.

The whirlwind of the so-called Diaper Decade in her early marriage had surprised her not only with its difficulties and joys but also with its boredom. As someone who always pushed herself to do more, be more, she was at first at a loss when it came to accommodating the nap schedules of babies and the distractible natures of toddlers. But, like every other challenge in her life, Carolyn not only rose to it but also moved beyond it, pushing herself and her children to achieve more and more. Whether it was baby sign language or mastering multiplication tables, Carolyn made sure everyone did more than what was expected and did it well.

Now, though, her youngest was in kindergarten, and Carolyn wasn't sure what to do next. She spent her days running kids to and from school and activities, squeezing in her hours for her full-time job between things. Really, the busyness of life had increased exponentially since the birth of her first child, but being busy didn't seem to be what she was looking for. No matter how full her life was there was still something missing. Even though she attended church every week, read her scriptures and prayed daily, had family home evening, and fulfilled her calling, she still felt a creeping emptiness. She went on dates with her husband every other week and enjoyed cheering her kids on at every recital and game, but there was always something squeezing in her chest making it hard to enjoy the moment. Sometimes the feeling would follow her to bed and wake her up at night with worry.

When Carolyn came to me, she appeared well manicured but exhausted. Sitting up straight in her chair, her hands folded neatly in her lap, she looked at me expectantly. She was here to get the job done, no matter how hard it would be. She asked me questions rapid-fire.

"James, I play by the book. I follow the rules. In fact, I feel like I've mastered the rules. Why," she said, tearing up for a moment, "why am I still so nervous? Why am I so stressed? The gospel is supposed to make our burdens lighter, so why don't I feel that? Doing all of this is supposed to make me happy, but I'm not. Why?"

Dave was, in many ways, a typical Mormon guy. He had served a mission, gotten married, and had kids. He was a home teacher and served in a variety of callings, from elders quorum presidencies to ward missionary. He was also like a lot of typical Mormon men in other ways, ways most guys didn't talk about at church.

Dave's parents were converts to the Church, and, for most of his childhood, happily married but economically unstable. When Dave was a child, his family moved a lot. He often worried about where his next meal would come from and if they had enough money for clothes. Even though his family was poor, they were somewhat happy, but that didn't change Dave's level of worry. Eventually, when Dave was in high school, his parents divorced, and Dave's father distanced himself from his kids.

Dave struggled for a couple of years and fell out of activity in the Church. He did come back, though, and served a mission. It always bothered Dave that he had a failed family, or at least what he perceived as a failed family. His family was not what you'd find in the Ensign, *and he always felt like less. When he was at church, when he was at school, when he was at work, he never felt good enough. He told himself that if he just chose the right, then his luck would change; bad things wouldn't happen to him any more. That was what the Church taught, right? If you did the right things, God would bless you. He thought maybe a mission would teach him that perfect combination, the right amount of service to make up for what he lacked.*

Dave's mission was mostly good but the worry and anxiety that colored his childhood still cast its shadow there. He struggled again after his mission with being active in the Church but returned after a few years and married in the temple. He finished college and got a great job. He and his wife had children, three boys whose presence constantly reminded him of how much he was needed and admired. They owned a beautiful home in a great neighborhood. His adult life was the complete opposite of his childhood. Everything looked right.

Unfortunately none of it felt right. Dave was always looking over his shoulder, wondering when it would all fall apart. He checked the bank account all the time. He expected (and often demanded) perfect behavior from his kids and constantly worried about what other people were thinking of him and his family. He hated it, but there were plenty of occasions when his wife and the boys wanted to go somewhere and he begged off because he was simply too nervous. Frustrated by the noise and chaos that seemed to be the natural default of boys, he began to find reasons to stay later and later at work so that he wouldn't have to deal with it.

When Dave's wife brought him into see me, they both looked pulled together at first glance, but tears threatened to fall from her eyes at any moment, and, despite his best efforts, Dave's stress was showing in his face and shoulders. Both of them were afraid to say it, but they were at their wits' ends. Why were they so unhappy? Why couldn't they ever unwind? Why couldn't Dave just relax?

When Lana first came into my office, she brought her husband, but now she was coming alone.

I always have hope for my clients—you can't be an effective therapist if you don't—but when she first walked in I had to dig deep for that hope. Lana seemed so lifeless. Don't get me wrong; she answered my questions. She was articulate and vocal and really wanted her life to be different. But no matter how forthrightly she answered the questions or how attentively she listened to me, she just wasn't present. Her emotions, her heart, and her soul were all absent.

Most of the time when she walked in, she arranged the chairs around my table so that she was sitting as far away from me as possible, and then she'd put a second chair between her spot and mine to use as a footrest, and probably as a boundary between us. Eye contact didn't happen often, as she was fond of staring out the window at the empty field beyond my office. As her twelve-year marriage unraveled, she moved her husband out, filed for divorce, and began to remember things she had been burying for more than a decade. She didn't always tell me everything she remembered, but what she did tell me made it clear why she needed to get divorced and why she was so disconnected. There was lying and anger. There was abuse. There was too much pain for too long.

She often scratched her forearm, worrying a wound that always got close to healing but she never could leave alone. She was losing weight, and the bags under her eyes indicated that she was still struggling with nightmares of her memories. We'd already been working together for several months, but things didn't seem to be getting better.

She didn't like to answer my questions. She knew that a higher power was needed to heal her, but she couldn't access it because, somehow, she knew she wasn't enough. She wasn't sure exactly what she needed more of, but Lana knew she was falling short somehow. After all, her life was a mess. That pretty much proved that she *was a mess.*

She had been a member of the Church all her life, and she had memorized the script: Jesus Christ saved us through His Atonement. She had taught this in Sunday School and to her children. She had testified of it over and over. She believed it. But now, when it came right down to her own healing, the pieces of the script would not fit together. The only conclusion she could come to was that she was falling short somehow. If she could just be good enough, she told herself, then Christ would heal her.

She had gone to church all her life, married in the temple, and followed all the rules—and her life was completely destroyed anyway. Nothing she had learned in church had prepared her for the difficulties she endured and the pain she felt. She was used up, worn out, exhausted, and damaged. What else was there for her to do? Who else was she supposed to be?

Identity: Big Questions and Big Answers

It's often said that the two most important days of our lives are the day we are born and the day we figure out *why* we were born. As spiritual beings on an earthly sojourn, we need more than just a physical existence. Finding out *why* we were born is what moves us above and beyond the physical realm. In many ways it is the key to our identity. To figure this out, we have to be able to answer the eternal questions: Who are we? Where are we going? Why are we here? We're usually pretty sure that when we can answer those, we will have found an extremely important part of ourselves. Perhaps even the most important part.

And when we can't answer those questions, we end up angry, anxious, and stressed.

Our theology offers us a clear and powerful starting point for the answers to these questions. It is phrased by Paul in his letters to the Romans this way, "The Spirit itself beareth witness with our spirit, that we are the children of God" (Romans 6:4). I have read this scripture more than once. However, the place I learned this first was in a song. It's one I've known for most of my life but have probably also underestimated for most of my life.

"I am a child of God / And He has sent me here," it begins. Because many of us learned that song when we were very young, we sometimes take the radical nature of its thesis for granted. But, really, what it's saying is amazing. We, every single one of us, are either a literal son or daughter of the Most High God. We are His children, and He is our Father. And not only that, but we are here on earth on *His* errand.

The song continues in its third verse, "If I but learn to do his will / I'll live with him once more." This part of our theology is probably less surprising to us. We believe (and sometimes desperately cling to) the idea that if we are good enough, we'll gain all the blessing of exaltation. We'll be reunited with our Heavenly Family and our earthly family to live forever in joy. It's a happily ever after tailored to our very own latter-day lives.

This idea is reiterated by the chorus of the song, "Help me find the way. Teach me all that I must do to live with Him someday." Being a child of God, we remind ourselves, means that we are meant for more than what we see in our everyday lives and therefore must be more. Unfortunately, sometimes this idea gets muddled and changed in the course of our everyday lives. Instead of helping us feel better about ourselves, this higher standard creates clouds of worry that wrap around us like storms with no silver lining.

Teach Me All That I Must Do (or Worry about) to Live with Him Someday

This muddled higher standard often takes the form of a spiritual checklist, something we can control and grade ourselves with. As we grapple with this checklist, we often just find ourselves worrying about whether or not we can check off all the items on it. This transforms into a greater sense of anxiety because it puts us, our puny mortal selves, in charge of whether or not we are good enough for God. So we worry more.

This worry was part of the script Carolyn, Dave, and Lana adhered to, and it is probably part of your script too. From the time we are little we are told, "You are Heavenly Father's child, and He wants you to come home. You've got to work hard, be good, rise above the things of this world, and then you can go back to live with Him and be happy." As we grow older, working hard and being good take on different meanings. As children, we need to be baptized and try to choose the right. As teenagers, the situations we have to choose the right in become more complex, but the standards are basically the same. As we grow older, we serve missions, accept callings, get married, and have children, but one day we are surprised to find that we are, as the scripture cautions us against, running faster than we have strength. We are doing all the right things, but we aren't happy.

Sometimes our lives push us past our own strength because of our own choices (like climbing out from under a mountain of unnecessary debt), sometimes it's just the way life is (like health problems or wayward children), sometimes it is our own sins (like the weight of gossip in our day-to-day lives), sometimes it's the sin of others (like a husband's pornography problem), or any combination of the above that leaves us exhausted and frustrated. We find ourselves feeling scared and alone. It is usually at this point we look at our lives and think, "What is going on? I've been told I'm a child of God, so I need to work hard and get back to Him. I'm doing everything I can, but it isn't adding up. Why am I so unhappy?"

When life's push comes to be more than we can shove our way through, we discover the script we're working from isn't enough. Like the man at the pool of Bethesda, like Carolyn, Dave, and Lana, each of us comes to realize that we, alone, are not enough.

Falling to Eternity (the *Only* Way to Answer the Big Questions)

As the first mortals on earth, Adam and Eve were the first to wrestle with the Big Questions surrounding identity. They were the first to be separated from their Heavenly Parents; the first to have the veil placed on their minds; and therefore the first to forget who they were, what they were doing, and why they were here. Subsequently, they were the first to sin, the first to fall, and the first to experience shame and regret. They were the first to realize that they would never be enough.

Luckily, though, they were also the first to be taught the answers to the Big Questions and when and how to answer them.

Elder Dallin H. Oaks explained it this way: "When Adam and Eve received the first commandment, they were in a transitional state, no longer in the spirit world but with physical bodies not yet subject to death and not yet capable of procreation. They could not fulfill the Father's first commandment without transgressing the barrier between the bliss of the Garden of Eden and the terrible trials and wonderful opportunities of mortal life. For reasons that have not been revealed, this transition, or 'fall,' could not happen without a transgression—an exercise of moral agency amounting to a willful breaking of a law (see Moses 6:59). This would be a planned offense, a formality to serve an eternal purpose."[1]

The Fall brought about the many conditions necessary for our life on earth, and as Latter-day Saints we believe that this was a hard thing but, ultimately, a good thing. We believe that this life is predicated on principles of agency, choice, and faith. Adam and Eve had to exercise their faith and use their agency to make a choice. They made the necessary choice to partake of the fruit and leave the garden so that they could have children. Thus, they brought about life on earth for each of us.

There were other effects of the Fall too. The two most obvious were physical and spiritual death. Now that Adam and Eve had left the Garden of Eden they were able to become ill and die. They were able to sin and separate themselves from God. Suffering and work became a part of their everyday lives.

Of course, they also received the ability to feel joy and have a family. They grew in knowledge and experience. For the first time, they began to gain wisdom. It seemed a price well-paid, for as Eve said, "Were it not for our transgression we never should have had seed, and never should have known good and evil, and the joy of our redemption, and the eternal life which God giveth unto all the obedient" (Moses 5:11). Mortal life brought them fear and sorrow, but it also brought them true happiness.

Thrust from an immortal holding ground, Adam and Eve discovered a mortal presence that offered a path to an eternal now. They were fallen mortals who had to learn to navigate both happiness and suffering, subject to the regrets of the past and the anxieties of their unknown futures, but in so doing would also be given the chance to reach a higher potential. Mortality, suffering, struggling, working, achieving, one day at a time, was the how and the when to answering the Big Questions.

Time: Past, Present, and Future Selves to Answer the Big Questions

The Fall had other effects beyond spiritual and physical death, though. Once Adam and Eve fell, they became subject to the effects of linear time. One of the primary differences between our mortal condition and God's eternal condition is God's interaction with time. Time for us is linear. Time for God is not. We do not know all the details of how time works for God, but we know that scripture explains it as "one eternal round."[2]

This means that while we are constantly moving one direction in time, God is moving in many directions. We can only see and understand what is happening in our lives right now. God, however, can see what is happening in our lives right now, what happened in our premortal lives, and what will happen after we die. He can also see with perfect clarity what we did yesterday, two days ago, two years ago, and what we can do tomorrow, in two days, and in two years in perpetuity. This is how He has access to all three realms of time in our lives. Christ, as God's Only Begotten Son and Savior of the world, also has access to those realms.

This difference in our ability to see things linearly versus eternally also has an impact on our identities and how we answer the Big Questions. Seen linearly, through our mortal eyes, there is almost no answer to why we are here and what we are supposed to do with ourselves. Even more frightening is what happens when we know the answers to those questions but screw up. And so it is that not only are we subject to the worries and anxieties of our fallen mortal selves, but we also are powerless to do anything about it. Is it any wonder so many of us feel so bad about ourselves? We mistake the person we are right now, today, for the only person we have ever been or ever can be.

For many of us, the regrets of the past and the anxieties of the future have become our reality and as the past and the future dominate our life the present moment, the now, is crushed. Essentially, anxiety and regret have become our identity and the opportunity to participate in our now life is lost. We have annihilated our *now* because we are so fixated on the past and the future.

Who Have We Become? Who Can We Become?

A client of mine once told me about a magnet her mother kept on the fridge. It had a frazzled, middle-aged cartoon woman on it staring desperately into a mirror. The woman looked seriously alarmed and slightly frightened. The caption read, "Mirror, mirror on the wall, I *am* my mother after all!"

How many of us have had moments like that? One where we look into the mirror and are startled by the face staring back at us? How many of us have moments like that with not only our features but also with our lives? Have you ever stopped to examine your life and wondered how on earth you ended up where you are at?

Many of us are so pressured by the demands of daily life and the worries and stresses we face that we lose sight of the Big Questions, only to look in the mirror one day and realize we have lost ourselves.

In some ways it is this lack of a larger understanding of our identities that leads to most of the problems our world faces. If we all really knew we were children of an all-loving God the Father and we truly believed that His love and wisdom could take care of our past regrets and our future anxieties, we could simply be present now and practice goodness.

Though useless, many people have the feeling that if they worry enough they can somehow affect the outcome of future events, or, if they replay and massage the memory of a past event enough, it might change the feeling of what happened. Try as we might, though, no amount of worry can control the future, and no amount of regret can change the past. Though the past and the future are a part of us, we do not have the power within ourselves to access those realms. For better or worse, we have only the present realm in which to shape our lives.

Another Big Question: What Is *Now*?

Another way to look at God's relationship with time is to say that everything is right now for God. There isn't a past or a future, there is simply all of it at once right now. That makes my little mortal brain want to explode, but it is still true for God. So, then what exactly is the now?

The now is essentially the moment you are in. It's the things we write poems about and paint pictures of. It's the cry of a just-born baby. It's the smile on your son's face as he comes out of the baptismal waters. It's the peace and quiet of snowflakes covering the ground on a crisp winter night. It's the joy of the first view when you reach the summit of a mountain. It's the feeling of peace that the Holy Ghost brings when we truly commune with God.

The now is something that is hard to pin down because it is both fleeting and forever, but it is something we all experience when we can pull ourselves away from the demands, distractions, and difficulties of everyday life. This is the hardest thing about the now, being present in it, and not allowing the past and future to overwhelm it.

It's what I'll be talking about for the rest of this book.

For the time being, suffice it to say, the now is what you are doing in the moment, and learning to be present in it is the single most important thing you can do to improve your relationship with God and access Christ's Atonement.

This Life Is the Time: Why Does Now Matter?

More often than not, when people come into my office, they are seeking some sort of peace, some sort of pain relief. They are burdened with worry over their past mistakes, and they are anxious for their futures. Over and over I have to remind them of one thing. Your past is done, and your future is, actually, out of your control. You only have one thing that is really yours: this moment right now.

They usually look at me like I'm crazy, but the truth is that *now* is the game changer in life and in the eternities. It doesn't matter what happened before, and it doesn't matter what will happen next because we, as limited humans, have no control over those moments. The past and the future are the responsibilities of eternal beings, which we are not yet. So what is left to us? Is our quest for betterment as hopeless as our past regrets and future anxieties would have us believe?

Alma answered that question fairly clearly when he told us, "For behold, this life is the time . . . this life is the day for men to perform their labors. . . . I beseech of you that ye do not procrastinate the day of your repentance . . . for behold if we do not improve our time while in this life, then cometh the night of darkness" (Alma 34:32–33). Russell M. Nelson put it another way. He said, "Now is the time to prepare to meet God. Tomorrow may be too late."[3]

Think about it. The only place you can create a new memory is now. We do not have access to yesterday to create a new memory, nor do we have control of the future opportunities to make memories. The only place we can create something new is now. Unfortunately, many of us destroy our now because we are so fixated on the past and the future.

That's the difference between simply seeking relief from pain and actually being healed and whole, and it's actually the only answer any of us really needs when it comes to the Big Questions. When all we get is pain relief, we have to keep watching and worrying about our past mistakes and any problems that might crop up in the future, just in case a painful situation might occur again. However, when we are healed and whole, we let go of the past and trust that the future will work itself out. We can stop worrying about if we are good enough, if we are doing all the things we are supposed to be doing, and what if we mess up.

All we really need to do is be present now by loving God and our fellow man, and God will take care of the rest.

Notes

1. Dallin H. Oaks, "The Great Plan of Happiness," *Ensign*, November 1993, 72.
2. See Alma 37:12, D&C 3:2, D&C 35:1, Alma 7:20, and 1 Nephi 10:19 for more on God and time.
3. Russell M. Nelson, "Now Is the Time to Prepare," *Ensign*, May 2005, 16–18.

Chapter 2
The Rabbit Hole of Past Regrets

More often than not, when Lana came into my office, we'd talk about one thing: the decision she made to get married at nineteen. Raised in a solid LDS family, Lana had done everything "right." She went to church every Sunday, read her scriptures and prayed, she attended and graduated seminary, she got her Personal Progress awards, she didn't date until she was sixteen, she attended and graduated institute, and she even saved her first kiss until she met the man she was going to marry.

"If I made all the right choices then, how come my life turned out like this? I'm a thirty-year-old divorced, single mom. This wasn't supposed to happen to good girls like me. What did I do wrong?"

The only thing she could trace it back to was her choice to marry young. Lana believed in marriage. Even after her divorce she still had a testimony that it was God's plan for families. And that was how, after she graduated high school, she followed her leaders' council and began to focus on marriage. She was attending college and prayed often about the possibility of serving a mission, but when she met Mike at a family home evening activity in her student ward, she felt the pull toward marriage.

She told me the story more than once in therapy. When she and Mike first started coming in, I had asked them to tell me how they met, and Lana talked about their dating process and the decision to get married fairly often.

In many ways, it was a typical LDS story. They met in their student ward, dated for a bit, and got married. They finished school and had babies. He got a good job in his field, and then they moved, bought a house, and transitioned into grown-up life. She stayed home with the kids while he worked.

"I chose the right all along, just like I was always taught. Why is my life such a mess?"

And then we'd start again.

Her decision to marry Mike wasn't all that strange, but in some ways it didn't fit the Mormon narrative we're all used to hearing. For one thing, Lana never had that Saturday's-Warrior-*Circle-of-Our-Love moment when she prayed about marriage. At the time, she didn't believe that she needed it. She had prayed, and God had told her that if she wanted to marry Mike, then she should. So she did. But now that things had turned out so badly, she began to wonder about all those prayers and answers.*

Maybe she misunderstood the answer. Maybe there were signs along the way that she should have noticed. Maybe if she had been more righteous, somehow God would have told her not to marry Mike. Maybe if, maybe if, maybe if . . .

Part of the problem for Lana was that she was still recovering a lot of memories. Most nights sleep did not come easy, and when it did it was often punctuated with frightening dreams that showed her what had happened and why she was so miserable in her marriage. She would wake up in a sweat and shake for a while, afraid to go back to sleep. Sometimes she'd end up cutting her forearms to take away the pain.

In an effort to make the dreams stop, she moved her bed. She bought new sheets and bedding. The dreams continued anyway. More often than not, she would leave the bed bare and, because she was struggling to find time with her work schedule and taking care of the kids to get housework done, just curl up with the piles of clean, unfolded laundry that were all over her bed. It eased the panic a bit.

Second guessing her decision to get married led to second guessing any other number of decisions: the decision to have children, the timing of the children, the timing of the divorce, the decision to believe in God and the Church. Sometimes it even led her further back in time, and she'd start second guessing all her high school dates and the people she'd met in college. It was like a game of mental leapfrog, but instead of making progress, all she ever did was hurdle one memory to the next to find herself back at the beginning.

"When does it stop? When will I have all of this out? When can I stop remembering?" she asked me.

"I don't know. When it's done, it'll be done. You wish there was an end?"

"Of course! I'm so tired of all this. These memories that never stop, that make it impossible to focus, I want them done. I don't want to be stuck in the past. I just want to move on. Why can't I?"

What's Harder than Walking and Chewing Gum?

One of my clients was a big reader and often during college would read as she walked across campus. Whether it was a novel or the latest nonfiction title, she almost always had her nose in a book. One day as she was taking a detour through a parking garage and reading an old favorite, the crossbar to the parking garage exit came crashing down on her. It struck her directly on the head. She dropped her book and fell to the ground too. Shaking but mostly unhurt, she got back up and dusted herself off and continued walking—this time without reading. After that, whenever she came across that parking lot she walked around it rather than through, and sometimes she thought she could even feel the sting and clang of that heavy-duty plastic arm striking her head even though she was in no danger of being struck again.

Our pasts are often like that parking garage crossbar. We may think we are totally engrossed in what is in front of our noses but really our pasts are looming, and when we least expect it, it comes crashing down, often causing both surprise and pain. My client did what any person would do in that situation: she avoided repeating the mistake. But what if she had given up reading or walking entirely? What if, instead of keeping her focus on the task at hand, she had spent her time rehashing the day, the moment, when the crossbar crashed down on her? What if, in her worry and fear of getting hurt again, she took to always looking behind her while walking, constantly looking at where she had been instead of where she was going?

This is what many of us do when it comes to our pasts. Whether it be a big trauma like abuse or molestation or a small trauma like a fallout with a friend or misunderstanding with our spouse or children, we not only avoid the situation where the trauma occurred, we avoid any and everything that we associate with the trauma. Unfortunately, the only thing that avoidance does is extend the cycle of memory and regret. Ironically, the more we avoid facing our pasts, the more we end up fixating on them.

It is a common joke that walking while chewing gum is difficult task for some people, but so many of us spend most of our lives doing something much, much harder: trying to walk forward while constantly gazing at the past. Not only is it almost impossible to move on if you're always looking back, but it also often brings pain.

The Neuroscience of Regret

If it is so hard for us to move forward while looking back, why do we all do it? Regret and its relationship to our lives is both a physical and a spiritual process. Let's look at the physical process first because a lot of how regret happens in our lives comes from the way we are biologically wired.

Through science we have come to discover much about our brains, and it is apparent there is much more to be learned. One thing we do know is that we have two basic parts to our brains: the primal brain (the part of the brain that is located near the back and just above the brainstem, called the cerebellum) and the higher-thinking and reasoning brain (the frontal lobe, located in the front of the brain). We spend most of our lives trying to wire the primal part of the brain to the higher-thinking brain because each of these brains serves an important purpose. They have to work together for us to function as humans.

The primal brain is commissioned with keeping us safe and alive. This is the part of the brain that keeps our lungs breathing and our hearts beating without thinking. It is also the place where fear is stored. The fight-or-flight or the freeze-fall-asleep[1] responses, along with anger, also happen here. Studies over the last decades have shown that our brains work hard to remember threats (presumably to keep us alive) and actually encode fear-inducing experiences into our neurons.

However, this process doesn't just apply to dog bites or other physical threats. Any kind of negative experience, if strong enough, can trigger this kind of encoding. This is why you can remember clear as day the time you wet your pants in kindergarten but you can't remember the name of the book you left in the car. The kindergarten experience was shameful and triggered the brain to encode the entire thing in that primal part of your brain so it would never happen again. It is this encoding that, in part, fuels regret.

The higher brain, which is tasked with helping us learn, grow, and get our needs met, isn't silent during this process, though. Often the two parts of the brain will be in conflict with one another. The primal brain, sensing the potential for pain (emotional or physical), wants to protect us through fight, flight, or freezing, but the higher brain, sensing an opportunity for growth, wants us to push forward. It becomes a loop of our higher brain pushing us to work through our traumas and our primal brain reacting with fight, flight, or freezing.

For many of us, our primal brain is running the show. Unless you go through therapy or have other emotional training, it is what you are wired to do. Through past experiences of getting hurt, the primal brain has convinced the person that danger lies ahead in almost every situation and protecting ourselves is needed. Though this approach to life might minimize pain in the short-term, it ultimately leads to isolation and emotional starvation in the long-term. This would be analogous to my one patient giving up walking and reading altogether in order to avoid the pain of getting bonked on the head by the crossbar. Sure, she's safe from the crossbar, but her life will be severely limited.

Conversely, our higher brain doesn't want us to be limited. It knows that to get our deepest emotional and spiritual needs met we need to learn how to be vulnerable, be connected, and be safe with each other. It also knows that for our bodies to be healthy we have to let those traumas go. As much as we should respect our primal brain for wanting to protect us, ultimate management of our lives needs to be directed by our higher brain.

In essence, the higher brain needs fifty-one percent control of our life while giving our primal brain forty-nine percent or less. If we don't do this, life can become a fear-based cycle where protecting ourselves means building barriers, judging others, and using anger to push people away—not realizing we are starving ourselves emotionally, spiritually, and physically.

The Spiritual Effects of Regret

The spiritual process of regret mirrors the physical process of regret. We know that we are made of two parts: a carnal self and a spiritual self, and we suffer when these two parts come into conflict. As the previous section explains, it is also possible for these parts to be in conflict within themselves. The spiritual effects of regret are evident in both ways.

Our spiritual selves are made up of light—the Light of Christ specifically—and our intelligences. Scripture doesn't tell us much about these two elements. In the Doctrine and Covenants we find the most basic description of the Light of Christ and how it interacts with us, "And the Spirit giveth light to every man that cometh into the world; and the Spirit enlighteneth every man through the world" (Doctrine and Covenants 84:46). Then in section ninety-three of the Doctrine and Covenants we are told a bit about intelligences. Verse twenty-nine says, "Man was also in the beginning with God. Intelligence, or the light of truth, was not created or made, neither indeed can it be." These two scriptures tell us that our spiritual selves are chiefly elements of light and truth. We are literally made to bring brightness, honesty, warmth, sincerity, and a whole host of other virtues to this world.

Now we know that the world we live in now is not all light and truth. It is not entirely made up of virtue. In fact, sometimes scripture paints our world as a dark and bleak place. The word most often used is the word *carnal.* Carnal, to our modern ears, means something animalistic or inherently uncontrollable. It reminds us of lust and gluttony and pride and violence. The word *carnal* as it is used in the New Testament comes from the Greek word *sarkikós,* which can also be translated as "fleshly." It is the antithesis to the Light that Christ was sent to bring and that is planted within each of us.

When we were born, we embarked on the great journey to bring our spiritual and our physical selves together. This wasn't going to be an easy task. In fact, it was going to be impossible—which is why our Heavenly Father promised to send the Savior. Because our carnal selves are usually impulsive and demanding and prideful, we often mistake the process for one of rejection. We think we have to reject and deny the impulses of the flesh, and by doing so we will be amplifying our spiritual selves. But in reality we are meant to become like God, who is Himself a being of flesh and bone.

Conflict comes when we use our carnal impulses in ways that do not bring light and truth to the world around us. When we choose to use our hunger to overindulge or take food from others, it does not bring light and truth. When we choose to have meaningless sexual relations outside of the bonds of marriage, it diminishes the light and truth those acts are meant to bring. In fact, all of the commandments we have are given to us to help us interact with our physical selves in ways that bring light and truth. Our covenants are given to us so that we can see a clear path to joining the spiritual and the physical and amplify the light and truth God planted in us. The primary drive of our spirits is to bring our spirits and our bodies into a unified state, and everything God gives us is to aid in that process.

When we act in ways that sunder our physical-spiritual connection, whether through letting the carnal drives in us run amok or by denying them completely, it cuts us off from ourselves and from God. We feel lost, scared, sad, alone. We might get angry and vengeful. We often feel a heightened sense of stress and anxiety. Mostly it is an underlying sense of unease, a lack of balance that sometimes fuels further sundering of the bridge between the physical and the spiritual.

It is what we call regret.

The Rabbit Hole of Regret

Regret is a basic feeling of disappointment over how something turned out. Regret can vary in intensity depending on the given event. Some regrets (like burning your toast) are small, while others (like losing your temper with a loved one) are big.

For many people their past is filled with and defined by their regrets. Like a magnetic pull, every day their past is lived over and over. They mistakenly believe that the best way to avoid future pain is to examine the past and find all the reasons something went wrong. They might do it so often that they don't even realize they are doing it. There are three main problems with this.

First, like a car spinning its tires in a ditch, this is a waste of energy. The truth is this: no matter how much time you spend examining your past, what's done is done. You cannot change the past by rehashing it. All that does is deplete your energy to be present now.

Second, instead of empowering us to make real change, hyper focusing on the past distracts us from the only place and time we can actually make a difference: the moment we are actually living in. The more we worry about the past, the more opportunities we lose to teach our children, to enjoy time with our loved ones, to excel at work, to enjoy life, to become who we are meant to be.

Third, this kind of anxiety disconnects us from Jesus Christ. Our Savior desires to make us whole, to bring our spiritual and physical selves into alignment. If we are wrapped up in our pasts, we lose the opportunities He is giving us in this now to grow and learn and become better. Going over our pasts, especially the painful parts, is analogous to pulling off a bandage and picking at the scab of a wound. Christ can't heal our hearts and relieve us of the burden of our sins and mistakes if we won't leave the wound alone.

Many of us feel about regret the same way Alice felt when she went down the rabbit hole. We find it to be a never-ending fall down a slippery slope that lands us in a strange world where nothing makes sense. This fall doesn't just lead to regret but also to its close emotional relatives: shame and guilt.

The Slippery Slope of Shame and the Foothold of Guilt

The wiring of our brains and the primary drive of our spirits to reconcile our spirituality with our physicality propel us to reexamine painful things, but the immediate effects of this reexamination are not usually healing. Usually the immediate effect is shame and guilt.

In order to understand how these different psychological forces work in our lives, we need to define them. Even though many of us use these two words interchangeably, psychologically and spiritually speaking, these two emotional states are very different and lead people down different paths.

From a psychological perspective, guilt is the feeling that you have done something wrong. Shame, however, is the feeling that you have done something wrong and therefore you *are* something wrong. Did you see the difference? Guilt is an external state and shame is something internalized. Guilt reflects your circumstances, but shame reflects your very nature. Shame is a slippery slope to a never-ending fall down a dark abyss. Guilt is a foothold to pull yourself out of a hole you've fallen into.

One common example of this is with weight loss. Almost every American at one time or another has set the goal to lose weight. That goal is neither good nor bad, it just is. However, some people choose to moralize this goal. They define the food around them as either good or bad and then, depending on how well they follow their diet, they themselves become either good or bad. For example, most diets don't allow for donuts. If a dieter were to go to work and see donuts on the break room table and eat one they might feel guilt and think, "Well, now I've undermined my goal. Eating that donut didn't make me healthier." That's guilt. However, most of us, because of the moralizing that happens with diets, take it one step further, "I'm so stupid! Why did I eat that donut? Now I will always be fat. Ugh. I'm so disgusting." That's shame. Eating the donut wasn't just an ineffective choice you made; it made you a bad person.

This is an important distinction and bears repeating: guilt is the feeling you have when you have *done* something wrong. Shame is the feeling that you *are* something wrong. More often than not, when we are hyper focused on our pasts it is shame that is fueling it. Guilt propels us to go forward. Shame convinces us to hide and wallow in our pasts.

The Spiritual Nature of Guilt and Shame

Guilt is actually an important part of our spiritual processes, but shame is not. There is no way for any of us to avoid mistakes or sins entirely. Whether through our own actions or the actions of those around us, bad things will happen and we will need healing. That's why our loving Heavenly Father provided a Savior for us. Guilt, when used appropriately, is a vital part of the healing process.

In his April 2013 general conference talk, Elder David Bednar explained the function of guilt this way, "The Savior is often referred to as the Great Physician, and this title has both symbolic and literal significance. All of us have experienced the pain associated with a physical injury or wound. When we are in pain, we typically seek relief and are grateful for the medication and treatments that help to alleviate our suffering. Consider sin as a spiritual wound that causes guilt or, as described by Alma to his son Corianton, 'remorse of conscience' (Alma 42:18). Guilt is to our spirit what pain is to our body—a warning of danger and a protection from additional damage. From the Atonement of the Savior flows the soothing salve that can heal our spiritual wounds and remove guilt."[2]

The story of Adam and Eve illustrates this in an in-depth way. Through the book of Genesis, the book of Moses, and through our temple knowledge, we see that regret, guilt, and shame have a long history with the human race. They had a powerful effect on even the first man and woman who lived on earth. It all started in the Garden of Eden.

In the garden, Adam and Eve were given two commandments. One was to have children, and the other was to avoid partaking of the fruit of the Tree of Knowledge of Good and Evil. We all know how the story goes: Eve is beguiled by the serpent Lucifer and transgresses God's law by eating the fruit. Adam follows suit so that he and Eve can stay together and fulfill God's first commandment.

Now, what does this have to do with guilt and shame? Upon partaking of the fruit of the Tree of Knowledge of Good and Evil, Adam and Eve experience regret for the first time. In fact, it would seem that even though they understood the imperative nature of God's commandment to multiply and replenish the earth, after eating the fruit they immediately began to experience personal guilt for the first time. Guilt, it would seem, was one of the first steps to gaining wisdom.

The scriptural account tells us that Lucifer, who in his baseness understands the foibles of human nature incredibly well, saw his opportunity to manipulate them and immediately began to twist their guilt into shame. Adam and Eve knew they had done something wrong. Lucifer worked hard to convince them that they had *become* something wrong.

However, due to their eternal identities of children of their Heavenly Father, Adam and Eve were not predisposed to wallowing in shame. In fact, we read in Genesis chapter two, when Adam and Eve were created, "they were both naked, the man and his wife, and were not ashamed." Up until that point they coexisted in the garden in complete openness and vulnerability. Their light and truth was unrestrained. As they made choices and gained experience, which was the only way to fulfill God's first commandment and for them to gain wisdom and progress, they experienced guilt.

Adam and Eve's first response to their newly discovered knowledge was an act of responsibility. Once they realized what nakedness was and what it meant, they sought to remedy the situation. That was the propelling nature of guilt motivating them to action. However, Lucifer, as we are told in other accounts of the story, interjected himself into their process and compelled them to hide. He wanted them to believe that because they had made a choice they were now fundamentally different and less valuable. He wanted them to feel shame.

It's the same thing in our lives today. We are often in positions where we make mistakes or sin or where the effects of other people's choices bring pain and suffering into our lives. Guilt comes from things we have done and things that have happened to us. But, when it comes to guilt from sin, we need to remember there are only two kinds of sin: sins we have repented for and sins we have not repented for. These are the events that often cause regret, at which point we often feel guilt. This guilt will propel us to find healing through repentance (often in concert with the neurobiological processes we talked about earlier).

Guilt will tell us that we have made a choice that is not in keeping with our eternal identities as children of God and that we need to act. Shame, however, will tell us when we make a mistake or sin that we have lost our right to be children of God, that we have to keep it all a secret, that our fundamental natures have changed, that we *are* our sins and mistakes.

This is especially true for those that have been sinned against in serious ways. Shame has an incredibly strong hold on those who have been abused in any way. Abuse, in all its varieties, is at its core a shameful thing. Abuse cannot exist without shame and, in fact, relies on it to thrive. Those who have been abused often internalize a searing sense of shame. This shame is markedly different from the shame that is felt by those whose shame is brought on by their own mistakes and sins. This shame is often deeply rooted and very persuasive. If you are a victim of abuse, whether it be emotional, physical, or sexual, know that the shame you feel is a lie, and reach out. Therapy or other types of professional help are often necessary to help you shake off the shame. God does not want you to feel that shame. Your Father in Heaven knows that you are not something bad simply because bad things happened to you. You are still one of His most valued children regardless of what someone did to you. His plan is for you to leave all that behind and to feel the enormity and peace of His love.

The Divine Disabled List

Thankfully, in the garden Adam and Eve chose to reconcile with God, and shame did not derail their lives. They confessed to their Father what happened, and together they came up with a plan to move forward. That process is easier said than done for most of us. If we aren't careful, we can end up seriously emotionally and spiritually disabled.

Often a person will recognize that their past is controlling them because they are constantly returning to thoughts of their sins or the bad things that happened to them or simply replaying over and over the stupidities of the day. By doing this, we are beginning to define ourselves by the failings of our past. Lucifer doesn't need an active sin to make us feel guilt in our lives; all he needs is a little shame and regret from the past to make us feel unworthy to receive the grace of Jesus Christ now. This often puts us on what I refer to as the *Divine Disabled List*, or *DDL*.

In sports, when a player is injured, they are placed on the Disabled List (the DL) and are not able to play in the game. The player is still on the team, and they are at the game, but they are not able to play. This is what happens to us when we allow shame and secrets into our life and live in the past. We disallow the love of God, Christ's Atonement, to make us whole now. We are on God's team, we are at the game, but we are not on the field of play. In many ways this is all Lucifer has to do. He wants to get as many of God's players on the DDL as he can.

Lucifer knows that if he can get us to create secrets in our life, he will have the toehold in our existence he desires. He understands that getting us to create secrets through the shame in our life will relegate us to the DDL. Then there we will be, on Christ's team, at the game, but we are on the sideline, unable to participate or receive what our Heavenly

Father wishes us to have: His love, His joy, and His companionship. Opportunities for growth and progress will be missed even if we've stopped sinning because our shame won't allow us to get off the bench.

This is the pivotal nature of guilt. When faced with guilt, we have the choice to either fall into shame and follow the discouraging path of secrets and sadness. Or we can choose to let our guilt guide us to the place of accountability. It is in that accountability that we find the difference between guilt and shame, the difference between light and darkness, and the difference between God and Satan.

Learning from Lot's Wife

How do we reconcile the two parts of our brains? How do we choose a productive guilt model and not get lost in shame and regret that will damage our spirituality? Many of us, like Lana, get lost in our regret. Our past decisions, mistakes, and sins haunt us like ghosts and lead us down strange paths until we are so mixed up we can't tell our good decisions from our bad ones. All we can do is watch our backs, losing sight of everything else. This is a particularly dysfunctional way of reconciling the competing needs in our minds and will only perpetuate the cycle.

In a 2009 Brigham Young University devotional, Elder Jeffrey R. Holland spoke about one of Christ's shortest admonitions to His disciples: "Remember Lot's wife" (Luke 17:32). Lot's wife isn't one that we as Latter-day Saints think about often. After all, she isn't a good example of any particular virtue, nor is her story flashy enough to be one that stays in our minds. However, as Elder Holland reminds us, Christ Himself has asked us to remember her, and so her story bears some considering. Given the multitude of scriptures stories and concepts Christ could have drawn our attention to, why did He choose Lot's wife? What is so important about her that the Savior of the world would remind us of her?

Lot and his wife were told to leave Sodom and, interestingly, not look back. "Escape for thy life; look not behind thee . . . except thou be consumed" (Genesis 19:17). Lot did as commanded and kept moving, escaping into a new city as the sun rose. His wife, however, did not, and it literally paralyzed her. The scriptures are fairly concise on her fate. They say, "But his wife looked back from behind him, and she became a pillar of salt" (Genesis 19:26).

In some of our rougher moments we feel a lot like what I imagine Lot's wife must have felt like as a pillar of salt: stuck, exposed, useless. In many ways Lot's wife is the ultimate metaphor for lost potential. Salt, especially in great quantities, was extremely useful and important in the ancient world. It lent flavor to food. It acted as a preservative. Some cultures used it as currency for bartering. But that day, on the plains outside Sodom, Lot's wife became something much less valuable than a human. And what she became in turn (salt) then became something much less than it could have otherwise been. It became dust.

This is what happens when we become obsessed with re-examining our pasts, asking, "What if?" And this is the same regret trap many of us get caught in, albeit in somewhat less dramatic ways.

Elder Holland put it this way: "There is something in us, at least in too many of us, that particularly fails to forgive and forget earlier mistakes in life—either mistakes we ourselves have made or the mistakes of others. That is not good . . . it stands in terrible opposition to the grandeur and majesty of the Atonement of Christ."[3] Not only does regret keep us from moving forward, but it also keeps us from Christ.

Moving Forward or Looking Back: The Difference between Faith and Fear

A big motivator to relive the past is fear of being traumatized again. The pain of our pasts make us ache so deeply that we would (rightly) do anything to avoid being in that situation again. However, instead of preparing us for a brighter future, our continual what-ifs only set us up for more failure. We don't end up with new perspectives. We only find things we already know being perpetually rearranged.

The way out for each of us is the same as it was for Adam and Eve and the same as it could have been for Lot's wife had she not insisted on looking back. We need to look forward. We need faith.

In the conflict between fear and faith we discover the battleground for the human soul. Christ understands this battle and lovingly pleads with us to maintain the highest values and standards even if we are unable to align our actions fully with Him right now. Through His Atonement, we will be able to overcome all things. When our Father in Heaven asked us to grow and become like Jesus, He anticipated our failings and planned for those events through His Son's atoning blood.

It is through our experiences we learn the good from the evil, and it is only through Christ that we can reconcile our sins, mistakes, and experiences with our hopes and our dreams—our primal brains with our higher brains, and our spiritual selves with our earthly selves. We should not be embarrassed that we need to call upon the Lord to save us from our sins, fears, and shortcomings but be honored to be in a partnership with Him. Jesus does not want us to have high standards so He can belittle us when we fall short. He doesn't want to shame us, nor does He want us to belittle ourselves. He gave us high standards so that He can aid us in reaching those goals through His loving Atonement in each and every moment. When we become wrapped up in regret, we disallow His love, light, and mercy in our lives. It is then that He will have to judge us, not as sinners but as faithless Christians.

As Elder Holland said, "And when we have learned what we need to learn and have brought with us the best that we have experienced, then we look ahead, we remember that *faith is always pointed toward the future.*"[4]

Notes

1. While less well-known than the fight-or-flight response, our bodies actually sometimes choose another option when a threat is perceived. This is the freeze-fall-asleep response. It's like choosing to play dead when chased by a predator instead of fighting back. In regular life, this response manifests as getting overwhelmed with sleepiness during an argument or freezing up during an abusive situation instead of fighting back. This response is automatic, and people often have very little choice about when and how this happens.
2. David A. Bednar, "We Believe in Being Chaste," *Ensign*, May 2013, 44.
3. Jeffery R. Holland, "'Remember Lot's Wife': Faith Is for the Future" (Brigham Young University devotional, January 13, 2009), speeches.byu.edu.
4. Ibid.

Chapter 3

Of Mountains, Molehills, and the Pests of Future Anxieties

Carolyn described a usual day in her life like this. She woke up early, around 4:45 a.m. First thing she did was turn off her alarm and check her email. Then she would pray and read scriptures and set up her to-do list for the day. She had an elaborate system of Post-it notes and alarms on her phone to make sure she didn't miss anything. Then she'd work from about 5:15 to 6:15, when she got her oldest son up for seminary. He'd spend the next fifteen minutes making himself presentable, and she'd wake up the other kids so they could all pray before he and her husband left at 6:35. After family prayer the other kids would get dressed and eat breakfast.

Then the day really took off. She'd answer emails while "nagging" the kids to keep on task. By 7:45 she was sending the middle schooler out the door to walk with his friends, and by 8:15 the elementary students were in the van and she was on her way to the carpool line. With some swift hugs and kisses they were into school, and she would hit the gym. She'd sweat it out for forty-five minutes—making sure to alternate her cardio with weights and interval training (she'd done the research)—and then head home to shower. By 10:30 she was making phone calls for work while cleaning the kitchen.

And so the day went. Carolyn had everything organized and planned out to the minute. She worked hard, her kids worked hard, her husband worked hard, and they got a lot done. Carolyn had it all together. Until you asked her why.

She came to me because she couldn't answer that question.

That question didn't usually bother her until she tried to sleep at night. There was the occasional morning where she would wake up burned out and just stare at the wall instead of the usual routine. However, it was most often nighttime that caught her. Carolyn would read herself to sleep. She was in the middle of seven or eight different books because she never seemed to finish one. She just picked up whatever was closest and read and read until her brain shut down and she fell asleep.

She often woke up a couple hours later with a start as her brain was frantically listing and relisting all the things she had done that day and what she needed to do the next day.

"I just can't seem to turn my brain off. I've read all the books and articles. We don't have a TV in our bedroom. I don't use any devices within two hours of bed. I exercise. But I can't sleep. My brain just wakes me up and keeps going over and over and over everything."

As we talked about this, some patterns emerged. Carolyn's nighttime ruminations seemed to center around things she felt she hadn't done right and things she was worried about doing wrong in the future. A tense exchange with her teenage son might get replayed in her mind, and she would begin to think about how the next time they talked she needed to do it better. A part of her brain would begin to think and worry about what it would do to their relationship when he went to college.

A missed phone call or appointment was even worse. Carolyn would try to guess the person's reaction and the consequences, often creating stories in her head with worst-case scenarios. Things like a missed Visiting Teaching appointment had her worrying that the sister would go inactive. A missed call from a client had her afraid of losing the contract.

The only solution for Carolyn was to get up and start making lists. She'd write out a big picture to-do list and then break it down into daily tasks with deadlines. She'd enter it all in her planner and cross-reference it with her calendar. Then she could finally sleep.

But, even after all that, when I asked Carolyn why she was so worried and why she planned so much and worked so hard, she couldn't answer. She didn't have OCD or anything else that was diagnosable, and her life mostly worked—except for the sleep problems and the invading sense that things could fall apart at any moment.

All she could say was, "If I don't work this hard now, tomorrow will be a mess. And if tomorrow is a mess, the next day will be too. A week, a month, a year down the road . . . who knows what could happen?"

The Prevalence of Mountains and Molehills

When my kids were little, it never ceased to amaze my wife, Brenda, and I what would upset them. Everything from an untied shoelace to the wrong color cup or a missing blanket was cause for sadness and anxiety. When they were toddlers, these seeming tragedies would result in tantrums and tears but were often easily fixed with hugs and simple corrections. As soon as the missing blanket was found or the shoelace tied, the crisis was averted and they realized that their lives were not over.

However, as the kids got older, we'd see the same cycle with other things. When they were in elementary school, it wasn't a missing blanket but an unkind word from a friend or a lost soccer game. In middle school it was anxiety over an upcoming test or an embarrassing moment or a misunderstanding with a friend. These issues would result in what were basically tantrums for older kids. Sometimes they'd slam doors or get angry at us or their siblings. The refrain was always the same though: life was ruined because of one mishap.

As parents we often tried to give them a little perspective. We'd try to explain to them that this one fight with a friend or embarrassing moment or poor test score wasn't the end of the world. It was simply a molehill that felt like a mountain. It was a small thing that had tripped them up, but they could still stand up and walk over it.

When they were teenagers, we often heard the same couple of refrains when they were upset. Not only was their life ruined, but they also often liked to say, "You don't understand! This *is* a big deal!" It was as if they were saying that since we didn't panic and worry with them then we didn't love them. Often it took a good deal of calming and listening before they would realize that our perspective wasn't uncaring, it was simply less anxious.

Kids aren't the only ones who let molehills take them down, though. As adults we do this all the time. How often have you stressed out over a single email or forgotten commitment or miscommunication? Have you ever passed through a day and looked back only to find worry: worry about schedules, worry about a loved one, worry about a task, worry about tomorrow?

When we worry over the future, we forget that in many ways, whatever will be will be. We trade out our now for something that is always down the road. This means we will never reach our destination because it is always just around the next corner. How many todays have you sacrificed to the worries of tomorrow?

How many more days are you willing to sacrifice?

This Is Your Brain on Stress

Anxiety and stress in our bodies is often felt in our chests or our stomachs. When we are anxious, our chests feel tight, perhaps like a weight is pressing down on us or a vice is gripping our lungs, and our stomachs seize. Sometimes it's a small seize, like butterflies, and other times it is much bigger, like full-on nausea. However, the root of anxiety is somewhere much more complex—the brain—and it has far-reaching effects for your entire body.

When the brain is stressed out, our lower brain, that animal brain, begins to take over. A small walnut-sized structure in the middle of your lower brain called the *amygdala* kicks into gear. It's the amygdala's job to process, when necessary, big emotions. When your brain senses something stressful, whether big or small, the amygdala sends out danger and fear signals, which causes a cascade of effects throughout your body.

First comes the production of the stress hormone *adrenaline*. With it coursing through your body, your heart starts beating faster. Your pulse and heart rate jump. You start breathing faster. Your senses of sight, smell, and hearing go on alert, tracking any possible danger. Extra sugar and fat are released from storage in your body so every inch of you will have quick, ready energy to respond when danger strikes. This first phase happens fast, faster than the time it takes your brain to process whatever it was that put the amygdala on alert.

The next phase of the stress response is more prolonged. It basically puts your body into fast-action mode. Like the accelerator does in a car, when your brain perceives stress, your body will be pushed to go, go, go. This is when *cortisol* is released. While adrenaline is meant to be a short-lived burst to get the body out of danger, cortisol can actually stay and function in the system for quite a while.

Cortisol regulates a lot of things including the brain, and when the body is put on high alert it can stay in this state for a long time. When this happens, it changes the way your body processes blood sugar (making sure there is a lot of it readily available while simultaneously trying to keep those levels low). Cortisol also dampens the immune system temporarily.

If all goes according to plan, the stress should pass, other signals in the brain put the brake on the stress state, and the body returns to normal, or *homeostasis*. However, for many people, stress becomes the opposite of what the body intended. Rather than an occasional burst to move you out of danger or achieve a significant task, stress becomes the daily motivator that propels us from moment to moment.

This actually gets very dangerous on both physiological and psychological levels. Chronic stress puts our bodies in overdrive for too long. Our muscles stay too tensed, our hearts work too hard, sleep becomes difficult, headaches become common. We gain more weight and eat fewer healthy foods. Short-term stress often makes people less hungry but long-term stress does the opposite and many find themselves indulging in more and more "comfort foods" to mitigate their worries. In some cases our bodies simply give out from the constant worry, causing problems like adrenal fatigue or migraine headaches. These ailments are often accompanied by racing thoughts, distraction from daily life, trouble sleeping, and sometimes even disrupted relationships.

The Lies My Anxiety Tells Me

Anxiety is persistent in most people's lives because it is convincing. Short bursts of worry or anxiety serve to keep us safe, but long-term anxiety does not serve us. Long-term anxiety exists because somewhere along the line we choose to believe the anxiety. It convinces us that to be worried and stressed is just the way things are. Then the longer we stay worried and anxious, the easier it is to stay worried and anxious. Anxiety often persists in our minds longer than it does in our body, and then starts the adrenaline/cortisol process all over again.

Clients often tell me that once anxiety has taken hold, it is nearly impossible to shake it off. The anxiety and stress run their lives. It becomes the constant in their tumultuous existence. Eventually, they begin to believe they can't live without it. Sometimes this is because anxiety has become the propellant for their accomplishments, or they believe that the anxiety is simply a part of who they are.

None of those things are true, though. In their chronic states, stress and anxiety cease to be useful warning systems in our lives. Instead, they begin to lie to us. The more we choose to live with anxiety,[1] the more we buy into the lies that anxiety tells. These lies are often persuasive and insidious. It isn't until you learn to identify them that you can start to leave them behind.

Lie Number 1: If I worry, then I am in control.

I once had a client say to me, "I have to worry about the future! If I don't, something bad will happen!" This struck me as a rather incredible belief. This person had twisted worry into a mechanism that could control the future. Simply by worrying about getting into a car accident on snowy day, she could stop the car accident from happening. By engaging in stress about the dinner she was making for the neighbors, she could make sure they liked it. By being anxious over what she wore each day, she could make people like her.

This way of thinking had another bonus too. Every time the bad thing didn't happen, she was the one that stopped it with worry. It wasn't just that she could make the neighbors like her dinner better; she could also stop them from not liking it. It was nothing short of miraculous.

It was also completely unreal. Her anxiety did not actually change her circumstances. No amount of worrying could control other people's feelings or actions.

When I pointed out the way her anxiety was misshaping her thought process, she dialed it back. But the power of believing this can ruin a person's life. After all, if you can control the future, then *you have to control the future.* If you don't worry, if you aren't vigilant in your anxiety, then all hell could break loose and it would be your fault. Even if only one bad thing does happen, then, according to anxiety-fueled distorted thinking, that bad thing is *your* fault and you had better worry more the next time so nothing worse will happen.

You see what's happening here, right? The future will bring about good things and bad things, but if you choose to believe the lie that stress can control the future, then you will be trapped in a self-perpetuating and self-defeating cycle of never worrying enough.

Lie Number 2: I know you love me because you worry.

Worry has another interesting feature: like a whirlpool, it often seeks to suck other people into it. To bring themselves comfort, people will often recruit other people to worry with them by making them feel guilty if they are not worrying. The message is, "If you really cared, you would be worrying with me."

Think about the last time you were planning a dinner party. Maybe it was a family dinner or maybe it was a holiday dinner. Put yourself back in the moment when you realize it's crunch time. Guests will be arriving in less than twenty minutes. The roast is almost finished and needs to come out of the oven. The salad is only half chopped. You can't find your favorite shirt that you planned on wearing. You heart is beating hard, the kids are running amok in the house, and your spouse walks in the door. Immediately, you start talking about all the things stressing you out.

On one level, you are engaging in a stress-relieving activity: venting. When you have a million things building up in your mind, sometimes venting it out to a supportive person is all you need. However, many times we turn this sometimes-healthy activity into a worry cycle. This happens when you take it to the next level.

If you are only venting, you can let it all out, get a hug from your spouse, and move on. However, if you are caught in a worry cycle, you will not want to or be able to put the stress down. You'll feel stuck, like you need the stress, and (here's the real telling point) when your spouse tries to move on, you won't let them.

It's at that point the venting turns into a fight. It usually sounds like this, "If you really cared about this, you would . . ." Fill in the blank. In the case of the dinner party, it could be "be mad at the kids too."

This kind of stress becomes particularly destructive because while on the surface it may seem like you are trying to build a relationship, you are actually seeking to control the other person. Over time this will alienate the supportive people around you and make you, the worrier, more and more isolated. Which in turn leads to more stress and worry.

Lie Number 3: Worry means I am doing something.

One of the quotes I often use in counseling to help people gain perspective about worry is, "The reason people worry is because it makes them feel like they are doing something about a thing they can do nothing about." Fairly often our anxiety and worry for the future occurs over the day-to-day details of our lives, but many of us often focus our worry on big-picture things. This can be anything from a political or social situation to perseverating on a child's dating life or hyper-focusing on your weight. This kind of worry often brings on this third kind of lie: that worrying about the thing is the same as doing something about that thing.

Let's say, for instance, that you are worried about your weight. Like most people in America, you want to lose weight, and you've told yourself that not only will your life be better when you are thinner but many things that happen now are a direct result of your weight (regardless of whether this is true). In fact, you begin to believe that your weight problem is causing so many problems that it requires constant vigilance, and weight anxiety becomes a part of your daily life. Now, in every moment of every day it feels like you are doing something about your weight because you are worrying about it. But are you actually doing something? Does worrying about the candy you did or didn't eat make the calories different? Does worrying about how long you did or didn't exercise increase your health?

The answer to each of those questions is the same: no. In fact, increasing amounts of research show that weight anxiety leads to increased amounts of shame and stress and *lower* amounts of weight loss. It isn't the worry that is going to help you reach your goal. It's self-care. It's choosing to do things that create better health, noticing how good it feels, and then doing it again. None of which requires stress.

This kind of substitution for action happens all the time. We do it when we worry about our teenagers instead of talking to them. We do it when we worry about politics instead of getting involved. We do it when we have anxiety about our marriages but talk to our friends instead of our spouse. In each instance the worrying provides a small amount of relief but never actually solves the problem, thereby increasing the worry cycle.

The Truth about Mountains and Molehills

The truth is that anxiety actually works against us. It is *never* working for us. Anxiety and the lies it tells us paralyze and isolate us. There is a saying that goes, "There are two kinds of fear, the fear that keeps you safe and the fear that keeps you afraid." Anxiety and stress, especially when it comes to the future, is not the kind of fear that keeps us safe. Rather, they are the fears that keep us afraid. Just like my children's tantrums made all their problems much bigger, anxiety and worry take our small problems and make them bigger.

All three lies mentioned above have several results in common. First off, none of them solve your problem. They only serve to promote more anxiety and stress. Second, they steal your time and energy and divert it to more worry. Third, they cut you off from true solutions—especially those that involve the help of others and most especially those that involve the help of the Savior.

That is the most impossible mountain to overcome.

The Conundrum of Always Choosing the Right

Many LDS folks are taught from a very young age that the most important thing we can do is choose the right. The CTR emblem is the one that we as Latter-day Saints identify with from our earliest years in Primary. The song is one we can sing from our earliest years too. "Choose the right when a choice is placed before you."[2] This is a strength of our theology. It helps us to cultivate a mind-set that connects our actions with consequences—both positive and negative—and encourages us to embrace our own God-given empowerment.

However, sometimes some of us turn choosing the right into more anxiety and worry, especially about our futures as Latter-day Saints on this earth and in the eternities. What was meant to be understood as "In this moment I will choose something for myself that I know will bring me positive consequences" is warped by the lens of worry and anxiety into "If I don't choose the right in every moment, then my future is ruined."

That may sound a little hyperbolic, but think how many days you've had like the ones Carolyn lives, trying to plan the worry from your mind only to be tripped up by the unseen. Things that are actually fairly small, like what the children choose to wear on a given day or a single missed homework assignment or a botched visiting teaching appointment, take on massive proportions. These massive proportions for many LDS people quickly blend with our theology to take on eternal proportions, which only increases our anxieties. We forget that our Savior's goal is to help us become better than we were. Instead we believe that we have to be perfect, and then we can come to Him. We decide that it isn't only our activities that need to be rated good, better, best but also ourselves.

This kind of approach often leads us to more anxiety and worry, and we begin falling prey to the lies of anxiety and stress in a spiritual sense too. We end up telling ourselves that by constantly worrying about the effects our choices have on our futures, we are in control of our eternities. We tell ourselves that it is actually our worry and anxiety that is making us good, and if we stop stressing, we will no longer be good, and it will appear that we don't care. We tell ourselves that for Christ and our Father in Heaven to truly love us they need to see us worrying. Eventually we replace paying appropriate attention to our sins and weaknesses with worrying about all the ways we aren't enough. We forget the truly needful thing is to take small steps each moment to become more Christlike.

This is deeply destructive to our spirituality. After all, you may not be conscious of it, but when you engage in that kind of spiritual worry you are negating Christ. If you replace trying to become like Him with worrying you are pulling away from His grace, in some ways you are saying to the Savior, "If you really loved me, you'd worry too." This is the direct opposite of what Christ told us: "In the world ye shall have tribulation; but be of good cheer; I have overcome the world" (John 16:33). Christ's message is the antithesis of anxiety. He's telling us that He has it handled, so we don't have to worry.

And yet, we still do.

Anxiety or Accountability?

Worrying about the future is another mistaken solution, like the man at Bethesda thinking that the pool was going to solve his problem. It sounds good on the outside but is also not true, and therefore, seeking it will actually just delay our healing. Think about it—what pool have we assumed will solve our problems, and how long have we waited for someone to take us to that pool or the pool to come to us? The only way that man could become whole is by taking up his bed and following Jesus Christ, and it is the same for us.

While speaking with a woman at church, I asked how many weekend nights she sat up worrying about her six teenage kids while they were out on dates. Her reply was outstanding! She said, "Actually, I go to bed on time on weekends so I can get a full night's sleep. If something bad happens, I will be fully rested and more able to deal with it. If nothing happens, well, I got a good night's sleep." Now there is someone who was unwilling to sacrifice the now for tomorrow's worries!

What was striking to me about this was this woman found an excellent balance between the very legitimate fears for her children's safety and the less-real fears that would put all of her family into a more stressed state. The difference was that instead of worrying about the future, she decided to be accountable to the now. By choosing to be well-rested, by choosing to take care of herself, she was owning her decisions in this moment and owning them in the future by setting herself up for success.

This is the perspective that Christ wants us to have. He does not want us to sacrifice the gift of today for tomorrow's worry, anxiety, or fear, "for God hath not given us the spirit of fear; but of power, and of love, and of a sound mind" (2 Timothy 1:7). He hopes we will remember good has overcome evil, light has overcome darkness, life has overcome death, and hope has overcome hopelessness through Him. It is only through embracing Christ that we can let go of our worry and find the happiness He has promised us now.

Notes

1. This kind of anxiety is not to be confused with actual long-term conditions like Generalized Anxiety Disorder or Obsessive-Compulsive Disorder. While the following thinking can be helpful to people with anxiety conditions, it should be remembered that anxiety disorders are common and real and often require treatments including therapy and medication, just like any other medical condition would.
2. "Choose the Right," *Hymns,* no. 239.

Chapter 4

Don't Look Now, but You Might Be Addicted

Dave had another thing in common with a lot of Mormon men. He had fallen into pornography. Like most of his counterparts, Dave had seen pornography as a young teen but had also done his best to avoid it while still seeming cool to his friends. He'd seen it a couple times but never looked for it on his own. However, as a young adult, anxious and frustrated and curious, in a weak moment he went exploring, and it quickly got the better of him. Over time, viewing it became a habit. When his life got to be too much—too stressful, too worrisome, too messy, too complicated—he retreated into that fantasy world. When there were too many papers due in school, when work was too crazy, when his roommates were bugging him, he'd turn on the computer and tune out. He would often view the pornography and later masturbate until relief would come. Sometimes he'd spend more time on it than he meant to—there were even a few times in college where he spent the entire night on it—but he figured it wasn't that big of a deal because he didn't do it all the time.

Dave didn't tell his wife before they got married. While they were dating, he hadn't looked at it at all. He figured it was behind him, and he didn't have to worry about it anymore, so why would he worry her? He genuinely loved Cami and thought she was gorgeous. He married with a hopeful heart.

Unfortunately, his hope wasn't enough. It was true that "the real thing" wasn't at all like porn, but that didn't fix his problem. Being with his wife was good, but it was also sometimes confusing and frustrating. Because Dave had been sexually habituated to porn and masturbation, sex with his wife was not satisfying for him. This created a gulf between himself and his wife, which only increased his reliance on porn. In several unfortunate moments he had pushed her to try things he saw in videos, which she was not entirely comfortable with, again increasing the gulf between them. And, as life got more complicated with kids and a mortgage and jobs and bills, the porn became an oft-used escape that made everything disappear.

Of course, the relief was always followed up with guilt. Dave knew that this wasn't the plan God had for him, and he knew it wasn't going to solve anything, but somehow, in those truly stressful moments, it didn't matter. What mattered was that everything was too much, and he was powerless. He would cut deals with himself. As long as he stuck to pictures, it wasn't that bad. Or, if he only used it a couple times a week, it wasn't a big deal. The deals never lasted long, though. Even when he didn't want it to, the porn was creeping into his thoughts and eating up his time. Dave was at times frustrated, then angry, then scared, then hopeless. What was going on with his life?

When Dave came to me he wasn't ready to admit it, but what had started as curiosity was now a full-fledged addiction. He had tried the Church's twelve-step program, attending the meetings and listening, but he was hesitant to participate.

Even though he felt disconnected from the group, Dave still paid attention to the steps. The first step was about honesty and admitting you needed God to help you get over the problem. That was no problem for Dave. He knew the porn was wrong and that he needed the Lord's help. The second step was about having hope that God would help you. In his worst moments Dave wasn't sure about this, but he did his best to believe it. Third, he was supposed to trust God. Again Dave was good there.

It was on Step Four that Dave quit attending the meetings. For that step, Dave was supposed to "make a searching and fearless written moral inventory." It just wasn't something he felt he could do.

"I don't get it, James. I've thought through this. I know it hurts my wife and my family because it takes the Spirit out of our home. But I don't know. I'm just not going to write this down. It seems like overkill."

"Is that why you quit going to the meetings? You think it's too much? It doesn't apply to you anymore? You don't need help?"

"Well, no. I mean, I know I need help. But writing it down . . . just feels like something that isn't necessary." Dave looked down at his hands.

"Okay. Well, why don't we do that now then? You said you know it hurts your wife and kids. Let's talk about that. Can you give me one specific example of how it's hurt your wife?"

Dave got quiet. He gazed out the window and glanced at the clock. He rubbed his hands together. "What do you mean by specific?"

"Give me an example of one time you knew it hurt your wife. What did you do? What did she do?"

Dave stayed quiet. His jaw got tight, and he clenched his hands together. He was working hard to hold it together.

"I just . . . I know that she can tell when I'm not happy. And it makes her feel bad."

"Okay. How do you know it makes her feel bad? What does she say?"

"Well, it isn't what she says. It's more how she looks at me. I mean, if she'd actually say something that might help. She always leaves everything up to me to figure out."

I waited. In moments like this I often like to let silence do the heavy lifting. I knew Dave's thoughts and memories were doing more for him than my questions would. Judging by his face, his discomfort was growing and so was his anger.

After a few moments, Dave set his hands back in his lap and got ready to stand up. "Look, I don't think Cami would want me talking with you about this. It's personal, and we're not here to talk about her. Besides it isn't like it would do any good anyway. She doesn't get it. She doesn't care. She just gets angry and makes everything my fault."

"Dave, you look ready to leave."

"Well, yeah, I am. I mean, I come in here to tell you I'm making progress and don't need the group any more, and you start telling me that I'm doing something wrong." Dave stood up.

"That's not what I said. Dave, you still have time left. It seems that you really don't want to talk about how your porn habits are hurting your wife. I'm not going to make you do anything you don't want to do, but I think it might help you to talk about what's really going on. Why are you done with the group?"

Dave took a few steps to the door and glanced at the clock again. He walked back over to his seat and sat down, putting his head in his hands.

"She's making me sleep in the basement. She won't look me in the eye. She says she doesn't trust me anymore. The kids keep asking why I have to sleep downstairs. I can't think of anything to say, so she says that I'm testing out my camping gear for this summer." A few tears slipped out. "It's just so stupid. I'm trying, you know? And she doesn't care. She just keeps saying she

can't trust me anymore. She doesn't even know me. She says the porn changed me too much. Do you have any idea how humiliating it is to sleep in the basement of your own home?"

"It sounds like the porn is really having a negative effect on your wife and your entire life."

Dave was angry again. "If she wants me to stop, this isn't going to help. Humiliating me in front my kids is only going to make it worse. It's like the longer I sleep in the basement, the more the porn makes sense. I get that Cami doesn't like it, but she shouldn't treat me like dirt."

"Why do you think she doesn't trust you? Do you think doing the moral inventory would help you figure it out?"

Dave looked ready to hurl some more accusations but stopped. Instead he dropped his head into his hands and said, "I can't. The list is too long, James. I wouldn't even know where to start. I just can't, okay?"

Lana looked at her forearms, tracing the red marks that would soon fade into white scars. Then she took off her cardigan showing me the burn marks on her shoulder.

"It doesn't make sense, James. I don't know why, but for whatever reason, when I cut, the pain actually stops. Like, yeah, it hurts my skin, but all the pain inside goes away."

Lana put her cardigan back on and continued. "My kids don't know. Sometimes they see the marks on my arms and ask, but I just wave it off as clumsiness. At first I was trying to not cut anywhere my garments were, but then I decided it would be better to hide it from the kids. So there's some other spots on my ribs. Sometimes I don't even realize I'm doing it, until after it's done. But it's weird too because I find that I have to check that they're still there and it feels better."

She looked at me, "I don't know if that means I'm crazier than I ever knew, but it seems to help. The cutting. It's kinda scary though. I think I'm doing it more and more."

With her cardigan back on, sitting in my chair in her jeans and ballet flats, Lana looked like any other woman I might see at church. If I hadn't heard the words coming out of her mouth, I would never have guessed she was a cutter. After all, cutters were supposed to be disaffected teenagers with too much eyeliner. Lana wasn't that. On the outside she was starting to look better.

"How is the dating going? What was that one guy's name? The one whose apartment you went to for a movie?" I didn't mean for the questions to make her uncomfortable, but they did.

"Ummm, that's complicated." She pulled her sleeves down over her hands and balled them up.

"Complicated how?"

"His name is Jared, and I don't think he's a bad guy, but I don't know. It's like he just knows what he's doing. It's confusing."

I waited for her to elaborate, but she didn't. Instead she showed me her right arm. "After the movie, I did this." There were seven or eight short notches near her elbow. "I'm not sure why. But my head was just spinning, and so I did this."

"Lana, why was your head spinning? Did something happen?"

"He kissed me. Like, a lot."

"Okay . . . it's been a while since that's happened. Should we high five on that?"

"James! Oh my gosh! It's not like that! What kind of girl do you think I am?" She flushed.

"Okay. Then what was it like?"

She bit her lip and looked out the window. "I don't know. That's part of the problem. I can't remember. Like, I remember sitting on the couch, and I remember him putting his arms around me, and I remember thinking that was nice and leaning closer. I remember thinking that if I looked at him, he would kiss me, and I wasn't sure what I wanted, but I looked at him anyway." She laughed, "I sound like I'm seventeen. This is ridiculous. I'm a thirty-two-year-old woman. I've been married. I'm divorced now. It shouldn't have been a big deal."

"But it was?"

"Yeah. He kissed me, and my first thought was, 'This is kind of sloppy. That's a lot of tongue.' And then I panicked because I wasn't sure if kissing with tongue was okay or not because all I could think of were my chastity lessons from Young Women. But he really seemed to like me. And I kind of liked that. But then it didn't matter because a different part of me took over and we kissed more. And then I just kind of checked out."

I raised my eyebrows.

"I didn't sleep with him, but it kinda felt like I could have." She began picking her scars. "I mean, I just don't know. Like, sleeping with my husband was terrible, and this wasn't. It was fun. It was overwhelming though. And I just couldn't deal with it. After a while, I don't know, I guess I came back, and I pushed him away and swore. He immediately jumped back and stopped. He wasn't out to hurt me or do anything I didn't want him to, you know? I think he even apologized. But I just . . . I don't know. So I swore some more and left and cut my arm."

She looked back at me. "James, I've cut every day this week. At work, my boss was really stressed the other day and got frustrated with me, and all I could think was how I was going to cut my shoulder to make it go away. Then, like yesterday, when I picked the kids up from daycare, they were fighting and yelling because it had been a long day for them, and it was like the noise just built up in my head, and I couldn't take it, so after they were all tucked in bed that night I worked over my left shoulder." She shuddered. "It's getting worse. I'm not sure when it's going to stop, but it makes everything feel better, for a while at least, so I do it."

She stopped and sighed. "I think I'm in real trouble."

The Facts about Addiction

We have a lot of preconceived notions when it comes to addictions, and most of them aren't true. What's the first thing you think of when you hear the word "addict"? It's probably a man. He looks disheveled and haggard. He's probably a drinker and maybe even does drugs. He looks a lot more like a guy from a public service announcement than your neighbor down the street. Odds are that what you picture is someone very different from you, and you think addiction is something that happens to people that you don't know, and, while it is tragic, it is not a problem you or people you love deal with.

The truth is that in America addictions are actually very common. The most recent data says forty million Americans meet the criteria for addiction to alcohol, drugs (including prescription drugs), and tobacco. Another eighty million are what's termed "risky users." This means that they are not addicted but use alcohol, tobacco, and other drugs in unsafe ways that do cause a threat to public health and safety. Very few addicts ever receive treatment for their vices, just about 11 percent.[1] These statistics led one writer to claim that "addiction is America's most neglected disease."[2]

Those statistics don't even include other addictions, like food or sexual addictions. In two major studies in America and Canada, researchers found that close to 5.4 percent of the population was addicted to food.[3] The number for sexual addiction runs even higher. The National Council on Sex Addiction Compulsivity found that 6–8 percent of the population struggled with a sex addiction (which includes a variety of behaviors, from compulsive masturbation to affairs).[4]

Pornography addiction statistics are harder to come by because there is very little research done by organizations that don't have a vested interest in the market. Some studies show that 30 percent of all data transferred across the internet is porn.[5] Other data suggests that 4 percent of all internet websites are pornography.[6] Statistics regarding porn use can be equally confusing. One estimate from an anti-pornography organization is that forty million Americans consider themselves regular visitors to porn sites.[7]

No matter which way you slice the data, though, one thing is clear: there are more avenues to pornography than before, and the contents of those pornographic materials are becoming more hardcore than previous generations have seen. For those who find themselves involved in it, it can quickly overwhelm them. While this area of research is still young, there is sufficient evidence to show that exposure to pornography has an effect on the brain similar to that of drugs and alcohol.

Even if you aren't addicted, you are walking a dangerous path physiologically, emotionally, and spiritually by dabbling in anything that can turn into an addiction. As M. Russell Ballard cautioned, "Remember, brothers and sisters, any kind of addiction is to surrender to something, thus relinquishing agency and becoming dependent."[8] Walking the path of addiction on any level can lead to destruction. Unfortunately, it is a path that most of us don't realize we've started going down until much too late.

The Distraction to Addiction Spectrum

Someone once said, "Fear is the memory of pain. Addiction is the memory of pleasure. Freedom is beyond both." I love this quotation because it points to several important things that are often overlooked when we talk about addictions. First, that addiction and fear are intertwined. You often don't get one without the other. Second, to let go of your addictions you have to let go of the fears that fuel them. And finally, that most important point: it is only when you let go of your fears and your addictions that you find freedom.

Now, not everyone who drinks alcohol becomes an alcoholic. Not everyone who looks at pornography becomes automatically addicted. Not everyone who uses prescribed opioids is an addict. Rather, these addictions develop over time as the individuals come to rely on the substance to alleviate some form of pain they don't know how to deal with otherwise, and they move gradually along what I call the *Distraction to Addiction Spectrum*. This means that often individuals engage in behaviors that distract them from their pains, anxieties, and fears, and over time they become more and more reliant on those distractions, and that reliance eventually creates an addiction.

The fact that addictions occur on a spectrum of behavior is probably much more familiar to you than you'd think. This spectrum starts with simple distractions and stretches all the way to the most compelling compulsions and addictive behaviors. All of us engage in distracting behaviors many times every day, and, when we aren't mindful of how we're engaging in those distractions, there is a high chance they will turn into addictions.

Social media is a good example of how this spectrum works. Whether you're on Instagram or Facebook or Pinterest, the story is the same. Imagine coming home from a long day of work and errands and extracurricular activites with the kids. There is homework to get finished and there are chores to be done, to say nothing of dinner quality family time. You walk into the kitchen, and you can't even reach the fridge because of all the backpacks and soccer gear strewn across the floor. You turn around to see that the kitchen table has not only after-school snacks on it still but also breakfast and the remains of the morning rush to pack lunches. You glance in the pantry only to find you're out of spaghetti sauce. Someone starts yelling from the basement that the toilet is clogged. Again. In that moment you realize you have a choice: lose your temper and get angry, or give up, for just a minute, and come back to deal with the problem when you aren't so exhausted. You choose the latter and end up getting on your phone to see what Pinterest says you should make for dinner.

Settled on the couch with your phone in front of you, everything disappears. There's no more messy kitchen floor, no more destroyed kitchen table. You hardly even register the kids yelling. Instead, your mind is filled with clean kitchen counters full of brightly colored produce that are effortlessly turned into "21 Meals Even Your Pickiest Eater Will Chow Down On!" The well-manicured hands get everything done in a matter of minutes and then dexterously dish them up to smiling children whose hair is still miraculously styled. Voila! Dinner is served! You can practically smell the perfectly roasted chicken.

Before you realize it you've watched that same (fairly unrealistic) scenario play out over and over for twenty-five minutes. You feel more relaxed, and while you are still frustrated with the (very real) mess on your kitchen floor and tables and, well, everywhere, you're ready to try to deal with it. That's the magic of distraction in action. It gives your stress response a bit of a break so you don't boil over.

We often do this with toddlers and preschoolers too. They're upset they can't have the candy bar they see while waiting in the checkout line, so we sing and dance and distract so they won't think about it anymore. Once again, voila! Problem solved. It really is a familiar and often useful process that we all engage in.

However, sometimes we overuse distraction. Think about your teenager and his stress about an upcoming report and presentation. Instead of jumping right on his homework, he decides to chill for a bit first by watching some YouTube. That little bit of intended YouTube turns into an hour and then he's suddenly behind on his homework and even more frustrated. Perhaps you even reminded him after he'd been on his tablet for thirty minutes that it was time to move on, but he didn't heed you. That's also distraction in action.

This happens to adults on a bigger scale than the Pinterest-for-dinner scale. I had a client once who used shopping to help her deal with stress. On the surface this isn't a bad idea. After all, she was going through some hard things, and picking up a shirt or skirt or toy for the grandkids wasn't a bad impulse. It also had the added bonus of making her feel better. She was always more relaxed after shopping and often had some new gadget that she hoped could make her life easier. However, as her problems increased, so did her shopping. The good feeling from the gadgets and the shirts and the toys never lasted as long as the stress. Over time the trips to the store became longer and more frequent, resulting in some serious debt. Even when she knew it was hurting her financially, she had a hard time stopping. Her distraction was on its way to becoming an addiction.

The Problems of Distraction

There are lots of steps on the Distraction to Addiction Spectrum, and not everyone who engages in distraction will end up addicted, but even if addiction is avoided, relying on distraction can become a problem. Think about how much time you've spent on your phone or tablet the last few days. Think about how much time you've spent working toward your goals. Think about how much time you've spent with your family. The numbers might not add up the way you hope they would. Most of us find that we spend much more time than we realize being distracted. That is time we could have used to further our goals or be with our families.

The other big problem with engaging in distraction is that, much like you've probably noticed with your teenagers, it never actually solves the problem. With the cranky toddler in the grocery line, it doesn't teach him or her to self-soothe or understand the importance of priorities. With your teenager, it doesn't get the homework done. It doesn't clean the mess in the kitchen or get the dinner made. In Dave's case, the use of porn as a distraction didn't solve his anxiety issues or his marriage problems. For Lana, using cutting as a distraction from her emotional pain didn't give her the tools she needed to start engaging in healthy relationships. This bears repeating: distracting yourself from your problems can bring you momentary relief and reprieve from a difficult situation, but if it is relied on consistently, it can set you up for bigger problems in the future. And those problems turn into compulsive behaviors.

Most frustratingly, distractions, if used inappropriately, can pull us away from our Heavenly Father and what matters in life. Our first impulse in stressful situations may not be to pray for help or turn to a scripture, but hopefully it does happen sooner rather than later. However, when we engage in distraction, those spiritual behaviors become less and less likely. As Elder David Bednar said, "Sadly [some of us] in the Church today ignore 'things as they really are' and neglect eternal relationships for digital distractions, diversions, and detours that have no lasting value. My heart aches when a man or woman may waste countless hours, postpone or forfeit vocational or academic achievement, and ultimately sacrifice cherished human relationships because of mind- and spirit-numbing video and online games. As the Lord declared, 'Wherefore, I give unto them a commandment . . . : Thou shalt not idle away thy time, neither shalt thou bury thy talent that it may not be known' (D&C 60:13)."[9]

It's precisely because distractions cannot solve our problems and dull us to spiritual impulses that they become addictions.

This Is Your Brain on Addiction: The Physiological Effects of Addiction

I've talked a lot about the brain, especially the higher and the lower parts of the brain. Stress, anxiety, and fear are all experienced in the lower part of the brain. When those are running high in your life, your lower brain is also running high and tends to overpower your higher brain. In short-term moments of stress and worry this can be a good thing (think: when you child falls and breaks an arm), but over the long haul this becomes unhealthy.

We know that stress is bad for the body. Stress can give us headaches, stomachaches, muscle tension, sleep problems, digestive issues, and more. Having a high level of chronic stress is associated with obesity;[10] it can increase your risk for strokes, hypertension, or heart attacks; and can even have effects on your reproductive and endocrine systems.[11]

However, the effects of stress on the brain can be even more pronounced. A favorite saying of neurologists is, "things that fire together, wire together." This means that every time an impulse fires in your brain, it wires to the preceding and following events, creating a pattern. In terms of stress we see this in a stress response becoming hardwired into the brain when certain conditions occur. For Dave, this stress response became hardwired when he came home from work, when he saw his children, and even when he saw his wife. How the stress is relieved also becomes a hardwired pattern. The stress that Dave felt when he interacted with his children, for instance, only became relieved when he was able to isolate himself and have some time on the computer—even when he wasn't looking at pornography.

These hardwired patterns come about by the interplay of neurotransmitters in the brain. Neurotransmitters are responsible for relaying messages throughout the brain, and they have different jobs. Some of them, like epinephrine (the neurotransmitter equivalent of adrenaline), relay messages to get the body up and moving. Others, like dopamine or oxytocin, help the body slow down and feel better. When we choose to be distracted from our problems, we often engage in behaviors that replace the epinephrine-type neurotransmitter with those that are more dopamine-like. In this way, our brains cement pathways that create patterns of behavior that over time become automatic.

Many of my clients tell me that they never thought they would end up addicted. It seemed like a small choice that happened only once or twice but, eventually, they ended up feeling out of control and lost. Often they knew the behavior they were engaging in was not the best choice, but it was easy and provided potent relief. However, that relief came at great cost to their minds, bodies, and spirits.

Spiritual Starvation versus Nourishment

The only time distraction is a useful tool is when you choose to be distracted in a way that is good for you. Think about it in terms of your body. Let's say you're having a day where you just feel fat. It's been bothering you all day, and you are getting cranky. Now, you can engage the emotion (we'll talk more about that later) or you can distract yourself from it by either going for a walk or eating a whole bag of cookies. Going for a walk can clear your mind and boost the presence of happy hormones, giving you perspective and patience. An entire bag of cookies gives you a sugar rush that feels better for a bit but later causes a sugar crash and maybe even a stomachache that leaves you less able to solve your problems effectively. Both will take your mind off the feeling you are having, but only one leaves you feeling better in the long run, while the other actually exacerbates the problem. Just like eating a bag of cookies does nothing to nourish the body, when we choose distractions that are not healthy, we end up starving ourselves emotionally and spiritually. In times of stress our spirits and hearts often feel empty, burned out. We crave connection and renewal, but distraction provides neither of those things. It can fill you up with ideas and thoughts, but it cannot feed you what you need, like security and acceptance.

Think about Jonah and the whale. Jonah was a basically good man, perhaps even better than most since he was a prophet. God gave Jonah the assignment to go to Nineveh and preach to the sinners there. We know that this wasn't just any preaching assignment. Going to Nineveh meant confronting some of the most violent and idolatrous people known to him. Jonah was understandably stressed, and instead of facing his stress he chose a big distraction: running away to Tarshish.

Another example is the story of the prodigal son. The second son of a wealthy father chose to take his inheritance from his father and "waste his substance with riotous living" (Luke 15:13). He engaged in many distractions rather than live up to his grown-up responsibilities. For whatever reason, this young man wanted to avoid the work of his regular life and thought that leaving home and doing everything but thinking about what mattered most made sense. Talk about being distracted.

It isn't the kind of thing we usually talk about in Sunday School, but the truth is many of us identify with the prodigal son's journey. And maybe a little bit with Jonah's too. The pressures of our nows, the lives we are leading this very day, add up to too much. We feel underprepared and overwhelmed by the problems facing us and our families. We get discouraged and scared. We begin to feel like we are burned out—starving—emotionally and spiritually. Rather than delving into those feelings we distract and distract and distract ourselves. To avoid starvation and to escape the barriers of our fears, we voraciously gorge ourselves on destructive relationships and habits, trying to get our needs met only to find we are in pain again. Hopeless and hurt, we return back to our bunkers, waiting for the cycle to start all over.

Both Jonah and the prodigal son found out the truth about distraction though: while it ameliorated their pain for a little bit, it didn't actually heal them. They both ended up lost and starving. Emotionally and physically spent, they found that there was only one source that could heal them: a loving father who was ready and waiting to give them a second chance.

It is the same with us. When we choose to be distracted instead of engaging in spiritual practices that solve our problems, we end up spiritually undernourished. Our hunger and thirst become unquenchable as we seek telestial answers to our spiritual needs that only Christ can fill. Jesus Christ promised us that if we believe in Him we would never experience spiritual hunger or thirst again (John 6:35). How often do we act as if we truly believe that statement though? How often do we turn to other means to meet our needs? Ultimately distractions and addictions are problems not just because they take away our freedoms but also because they sever our relationship with Christ. And without Him, there is no hope for any of us, addicted or not.

Thankfully, addiction doesn't have to be the end of anyone's story.

Hope for Those Struggling with Addictions

An interesting set of experiments, called the Rat Park experiments, from the late 1970s, add further insights to the Distraction to Addiction Spectrum. In these experiments, rats were placed in two different types of cages and offered opioid-laced water. It turns out what mattered more was not the access to opioids but what kind of cage the rats were in.

One set of rats was put in a small, empty cage. The only choice these rats had was to drink regular water or opioid-laced water. These rats had basically nothing to do except indulge in the opioids. Another set of rats was put into luxurious cages where they had access to play spaces, food, and playmates. They were put into a community and given a large number of other things to do. In almost every way this second set of rats were put into a stress-free environment. They too were given the choice between plain water and opioid-laced water. The rats in the boring cage drank so much of the opioid-laced water that they became deeply addicted and eventually killed themselves. The rats in the stress-free cages, however, drank almost none of the opioid-laced water. They tried it because they didn't know what it was, but none of the rats became addicted, and none of them died from an opioid overdose.

This experiment points to how important our environments are. Sure, we aren't rats and can never truly live in a stress-free pleasure zone with our needs catered to. Life doesn't work that way. But, by the same token, how we deal with the stress in our lives—whether or not we are willing to reach out to the people around us for support—can make all the difference in how addicted a person becomes. If we, like the rats in the second set of cages, can structure our lives in ways that productively relieve stress, our need for distraction will never grow into a need for addiction.

Another big difference between our lives and rat lives is that we have a much greater degree of agency and knowledge than a rat does. This, of course, can cut both ways. The ability we have as humans to find, create, or expose ourselves to addictive materials is greater than it has ever been. However, that same agency and knowledge that can lead us to addiction can also draw us closer to Christ. It can help us create lives in which we learn how to not just pray for help but also mindfully embrace the love and grace our Heavenly Father offers us through His Son's Atonement so that even in the face of tremendous stress, even when we find ourselves at rock bottom, our lives can become a rat park. Not from the outside in, but from the inside out.

Because God has endowed us with agency and the Light of Christ, we are spiritual beings with characteristics of the Most High God, and as such we have another dimension and another source of power to create our best, most stress-free lives. This is the true purpose and power of the Atonement of Christ. It won't eradicate all of our difficulties or hardships, but if we are willing to accept Christ into our everyday lives, His Atonement can empower us to withstand even the most heart-rending circumstances.

Christ will give us, "beauty for ashes, the oil of joy for mourning, the garment of praise for the spirit of heaviness" (Isaiah 61:3). This is His promise to us as children of our Heavenly Father. He has suffered so we can suffer only as much as we need to in order to learn and grow. We don't have to be locked into our struggles only seeking temporary relief from the pain they afford. We can be given strength, perspective, patience, and peace.

We can be healed.

Notes

1. Partnership News Service. "New Data Show Millions of Americans with Alcohol and Drug Addiction Could Benefit from Health Care Reform—Where Families Find Answers on Substance Use | Partnership for Drug-Free Kids." Partnership for Drug-Free Kids—Where Families Find Answers. September 28, 2010. Accessed September 03, 2018. https://drugfree.org/learn/drug-and-alcohol-news/new-data-show-millions-of-americans-with-alcohol-and-drug-addiction-could-benefit-from-health-care-reform/.
2. Lloyd Sederer, "A Blind Eye to Addiction," U.S. News & World Report, June 1, 2015, Accessed September 03, 2018, http://www.usnews.com/opinion/blogs/policy-dose/2015/06/01/america-is-neglecting-its-addiction-problem.
3. Alan J. Flint et al., "Food-Addiction Scale Measurement in 2 Cohorts of Middle-Aged and Older Women," Oxford Academic, January 22, 2014, accessed September 03, 2018, http://ajcn.nutrition.org/content/early/2014/01/22/ajcn.113.068965.short. And Pardis Pedram et al., "Food Addiction: Its Prevalence and Significant Association with Obesity in the General Population," PLOS Medicine, September 4, 2013, accessed September 03, 2018, http://journals.plos.org/plosone/article?id=10.1371/journal.pone.0074832.
4. "Sexual Addiction and Compulsivity Research Bibliography," SASH, 2017, accessed September 03, 2018, http://www.sash.net/sexual-addiction-and-compulsivity-research-bibliography.
5. Alexis Kleinman, "Porn Sites Get More Visitors than Netflix, Amazon and Twitter Combined," *The Huffington Post,* December 07, 2017, accessed September 03, 2018, https://www.huffingtonpost.com/2013/05/03/internet-porn-stats_n_3187682.html.
6. Mark Ward, "Web Porn: Just How Much Is There?" BBC News, July 01, 2013, accessed September 03, 2018, https://www.bbc.com/news/technology-23030090.
7. "How Many People Are on Porn Sites Right Now? (Hint: It's A Lot.)," Fight the New Drug, April 02, 2018, accessed September 03, 2018, http://fightthenewdrug.org/by-the-numbers-see-how-many-people-are-watching-porn-today.
8. M. Russell Ballard, "That Cunning Plan of the Evil One," *Ensign*, November 2010.
9. David A. Bednar, "Things as They Really Are," *Ensign*, June 2010, 19.
10. "Why Stress Causes People to Overeat," Harvard Health Publishing, July 18, 2018, accessed September 03, 2018, http://www.health.harvard.edu/newsletter_article/why-stress-causes-people-to-overeat.
11. Steve Tovian et al., "Stress Effects on the Body," American Psychological Association, accessed September 03, 2018, http://www.apa.org/helpcenter/stress-body.aspx.

Part Two

RISE

The impotent man answered him, Sir, I have no man, when the water is troubled, to put me into the pool: but while I am coming, another steppeth down before me.

Jesus saith unto him, ***Rise****.*

—John 5:7–8

Yes, there are adversities to be overcome, not a few of them. There are trials to be endured. There is much of evil in the world and too much of harshness, even in the home. Do what you can to rise above all of this. Stand up. . . . Rise up in the stature of your divine inheritance.

—Gordon B. Hinckley

("Rise to the Stature of the Divine Within You," *Ensign*, November 1989, 94.)

Chapter 5

Atonement Now: Receiving Christ's Grace Yesterday, Today, and Forever

Carolyn's worry kept increasing. Most of it was about the usual things, but she was also now worrying about her husband and his choices the way she worried about her own. The more time her husband spent working on his elders quorum calling, the more she worried about the time he wasn't with the family. Of course, when he wasn't working with the elders quorum, she worried about all the people who needed his help. Then she resented the time he spent on his calling. This, in turn, became guilt. At which point she pushed herself harder. She had to be more charitable. She needed to be a better wife. She needed to be the best possible mom. She knew this. Her future and the future of her family depended on it. She had to choose the right, be anxiously engaged, and put her shoulder to the wheel so they could be a forever family.

So she did more visiting teaching and prepared more elaborate Sunday lessons. She smiled more and agreed with her husband even when she wanted to scream. She signed her kids up for more activities and oversaw their homework more diligently. She budgeted more and spent less.

But still, even after all that, Carolyn couldn't sleep at night. The evening attacks were more intense, and she found herself snipping at her kids and husband for bothering her for help with the very things she was making them do. Carolyn was smart. It didn't take her long to figure out her current life wasn't working. She knew that God meant for her to have joy in the eternities, but sometimes all the work it took to get to those eternal blessings made her wonder if it was really worth it.

Recently during her scripture study, Carolyn worked her way through the Sermon on the Mount. She loved the Beatitudes. They were so clear and comforting. Mourn, and you'll be comforted. Be meek, and you'll inherit the earth. Have mercy, and you'll get mercy. Be a peacemaker, and be called a child of God. That's how God worked. Do the right thing now, and your future was assured.

Of course, as much as she loved the Beatitudes, she was always rattled by the end of the chapter. It was like an extra beatitude tacked on after all the others. A simple yet challenging call to action for those who were truly converted to Christ. "Be ye therefore perfect, even as your Father which is in heaven is perfect."

Carolyn knew that when Christ had preached the Sermon on the Mount and preached to the Nephites and commanded "be ye therefore perfect" He didn't mean perfect-perfect. She knew God fully expected her to make mistakes, and that was why He had sacrificed His Son. After all, the footnote on that scripture told her that perfect in this case meant "complete."

But Carolyn couldn't shake the nagging feeling that there was more to life than what she currently had and that despite her efforts she was somehow still incomplete. Something inside her—some days she wondered if it was the Spirit—seemed to whisper that she just wasn't good enough, and she never would be. She would never reach the standard Christ set.

Carolyn, stalwart as she was, found doubt sneaking in. Some days there was a temptation to give up. What was the point? If she had to be perfect to protect her future, well, that was never going to work, so why should she keep trying?

It crept up on her at first, but one Sunday it was undeniable: Carolyn was bitter. She was mad at God. She knew she didn't have any real reason to be, but somehow or other the whole righteousness thing was starting to feel like a bum deal.

She believed in the Church, and she was sure that would never change, but more and more these days Carolyn sure wished she didn't.

It wasn't what Dave wanted, but now that his wife had kicked him out of the house he was alone a lot and found himself more and more tempted.

The porn was always there. It was always on. It was always available. It didn't matter that Dave knew it was hollow. What mattered was that it was there.

He tried to set limits. He tried to avoid it. He tried talking to his bishop. He even tried the twelve-step program at church again. None of it seemed to help. And it didn't seem to matter how long he held out between indiscretions. He always fell back into his weakness.

The worst was always the Sunday after. Sometimes the day after, the morning after, Dave could pretend that it wasn't so bad. He told himself that it was just one slip up, and he was going to move forward. But, then, when Sunday came and the sacrament tray came his way, Dave's heart would get tight, and he'd pass the tray on without taking anything. The longer he went without, the more his sin bothered him, and the emptier church felt.

Dave had been through the entire twelve-step program at least twice. However, as his wife pointed out when they separated, he didn't really participate. He sort of audited the group like he used to audit science classes in college. He would go and listen and learn a lot of facts, but things didn't sink in on a deep level.

Dave felt this was only partly true. He was really good at the first three steps. He knew his life was unmanageable. A secret porn user who couldn't be intimate with his wife and was constantly grumpy at his children was not who he wanted to be. He knew he needed a higher power to get him out of the mess he'd made. How many nights had he prayed and prayed for Christ's intervention and forgiveness?

It was step four that still tripped him up. The searching and fearless inventory was not something that was doable for him. Every time he started making the list of all the things he'd done wrong and the people that it hurt, he felt his head start to spin. Dave would sometimes get nauseous and struggle to breathe.

They were coming up on step four again this week, and he was dreading it. His worry over it was creeping into his work life, and he found it hard to concentrate. Finally, the night before the Addiction Recovery Group met, Dave sat down, his hands shaking with fear, and started writing. His wife's name was first, with a long list of memories that he was not proud of. His kids' names came next, and Dave was ill with shame. As he started to cry, the pencil fell from his hands.

"Father in Heaven," he prayed, "this is horrible. How can this help me? How will I ever be worthy again? How will I ever make this right? How can I make this pain stop?"

Lana was finished. In her soul, deep down where she knew there should be something, there was nothing. It was a pit. A vortex. It swirled and churned, and she never understood how something that was nothing could cause so much pain.

One night she had messed up—gotten overwhelmed, checked out, and had sex with the guy she was dating. In some ways it felt better than anything she had been through in her marriage, but in other ways it complicated her life. She wanted so badly to feel close to someone, to feel loved, to stop being lost. When she slept with him, it was almost like she didn't know what was happening even though she wasn't a virgin. All she knew was that for a little while, at least, she had all those things she wanted for so long. Of course, it didn't last. Jared never meant to stay; he wasn't committed to her. He cared about her and didn't want to hurt her but was also not interested in being with her long-term, which only confused her even more and deepened her pain.

More than she cared to admit, Lana thought about hurting herself. She was doing her best to stop cutting, but her life was stressful. The problems in her dating life only made it worse. Her two daughters were starting to ask more and more questions, and she wasn't sure how long she could keep them from figuring out what a mess she really was.

She was still waking up at night with nightmares and working to hold down a full-time job while taking care of the kids. She went to church every Sunday, sometimes leaving the meeting because her grief got the best of her. She'd sit in a bathroom stall and cry, sometimes for most of the block. And it seemed that the more she cried, the bigger the nothing inside her grew and the more pain she felt.

Finally, the pressure of work and being a single mom while still bearing the onus of trying to achieve normalcy was too much. Lana began to notice that separate from her self-harm thoughts was a new strand of interruptive thoughts. These were darker and more frightening, and in them Lana wasn't just hurting herself—she was ending her life.

The thoughts scared her deeply. Lana knew she didn't want to kill herself—not really—but she needed the pain to stop.

Sometimes she would pray at night, when she couldn't sleep. It was a simple prayer, one she could hold onto even when the emptiness and darkness inside her loomed and threatened to crush her. "Lord, make it stop. Just make it stop. Please God, make it stop."

Thorns in the Flesh

Paul, in his second letter to the Corinthians, wrote about his "thorn in the flesh." He doesn't say a lot about it, but it seems fairly clear that it was a long-term issue that bothered him immensely. In 2 Corinthians 12, he gives this brief description: "Lest I should be exalted above measure . . . there was given to me a thorn in the flesh, the messenger of Satan to buffet me . . . for this thing I besought the Lord thrice, that it might depart from me. And he said unto me, My grace is sufficient for thee; for my strength is made perfect in weakness" (verses 7–10).

Those are strong words from Paul, and they are words that most of us can identify with from time to time. Our weaknesses, our future anxieties and past regrets, are exactly that. Like a thorn in your hand, they hurt and nag. We know that we'll feel better once we get them out but, more often than not, we see no way to do it. Like Carolyn, Dave, Lana, and Paul, we find ourselves on our knees begging God that these overwhelming feelings—what we perceive as failings—will leave us. Sometimes our cries from the dark nights of our souls may sound similar to Christ's cry in the garden, "Remove this cup from me" (Luke 22:42). However, like it was for Paul and our Savior, our thorns in the flesh are seldom removed in those moments. God wants us to live through our tough times, to experience them, and as He told Paul, trust that His strength will see us through.

This is something we all know. Think about how many conference talks you've heard about enduring hardship well. This isn't a question of belief either. Usually we believe that Christ suffered for us. The question is never whether God will support us in our pain. No, our questions, whether we phrase them like Lana or Dave or Carolyn, are almost always *How? How*, we importune the Lord, *how will You save me*?

The Lens of Eternity

Paul, in his first letter to the Corinthians, wrote another famous and oft-quoted scripture. In chapter thirteen, just after his famous description of charity and the pure love of Christ, he wrote, "When I was a child I spake as a child, I understood as a child, I thought as a child; but when I became a man, I put away childish things. *For now we see through a glass, darkly; but then face to face; now I know in part; but then shall I know even as also I am known*" (1 Corinthians 13:12; emphasis added). Paul knew that even as he was maturing through his mortal life, there were things unknown to him. He looked forward to a time in the future when he could know things even as he himself was known.

Our past regrets and future anxieties are like that dark glass. Like the opposite of rose-colored glasses, they often color our perceptions, making our past mistakes worse than they really were and casting grim, cloudy futures before us. Looking through that dark glass obscures not only our minds but our hearts and souls too. Like Paul, our only hope becomes some unknown time when, somehow or other, we'll be able to see things more clearly, understand things even as we are understood by God.

Often, when we are struggling through our dark-glass moments, we tell ourselves we just have to look on the bright side. We try to count our blessings and reach for those rose-colored glasses, hoping that we can just spitshine our current worries and move on. This is good, but God has even greater things in mind than just polishing our fears and trying to skip over them. He has understanding in store. He has peace waiting for our hearts. He has healing, on every level, as soon as we are ready for it.

God means for us to have those things *now*. We can start to tap into that understanding today. We don't have to wait. We can swap out the dark glass of our worry and fear not just for rose-colored glasses of temporary optimism. We can embrace a lens of eternity that makes each moment as we live it not dark or rose-colored, but rather, varied, powerful, peaceful, and full of God's love right *now*.

Letting Go of Our Pasts and Our Futures

Being fixated on our pasts and futures is what we're taught from a very young age. We know that to be exalted, to become who God desires us to be, we must repent. That means thinking about our pasts. We also know that we have to choose the right. That means thinking about our futures. We have an eternal mandate to pay attention to and take care of our pasts and our futures. Thinking about the now can feel like we are not being responsible Saints.

Here's the thing to remember: focusing on the now does not mean we completely disregard what has happened before and what might happen next. It means the exact opposite, actually. Focusing on the now means focusing on what you can control instead of focusing on the things you cannot control. And, when it comes right down to it, there is only one thing you actually can control: yourself in the very moment you are in.

To do this, though, we must let go of both our pasts and our futures. Again, people automatically assume this means being negligent regarding our eternal responsibilities. Letting go of our pasts and our futures doesn't mean that at all, though. Instead it means giving control to the one person who has complete access to our day-to-day moments, our futures, and our pasts: Jesus Christ.

If we are to be successful in our journey toward becoming who our Heavenly Father wants us to become, we must be wholly reliant on our Elder Brother, who is mighty to save (Isaiah 63:1). Christ came to earth to pay for the sins, errors, mistakes, heartaches, and pains of all mankind (the past), and he also came to earth to secure the future of all mankind. Christ proclaimed in John chapter 16 verse 33, "These things I have spoken unto you, that in me ye might have peace. In the world ye shall have tribulation: but be of good cheer; I have overcome the world." Basically, Jesus lived and died then so that each of us can live *now*.

Some might ask, does living in the now mean discounting our past errors? Does that mean we abandon repentance? Again the answer is an emphatic *no*. If we want to discontinue the impact of a negative past the best place to do that is now. Now is the time to prepare to meet God.

This means leveraging our past mistakes into learning through repentance today so that faith in tomorrow can be restored.

It helps to think about this in terms of a garden. Your life is like a garden, and your hopes, dreams, and accomplishments are the plants in it. However, for many reasons (some of which are under your control and some of which aren't) weeds creep in. These weeds are like sins and mistakes—past regrets. Now, you can pull those weeds out and spray them with herbicide, and some of them will keep coming back. So you'll pull and work, and with time and effort, your garden will be weed free. This is like repentance.

Now would it make any sense, as Elder Neal A. Maxwell was fond of asking, to go about "pulling up the daisies to see how the roots are doing"?[1] What would happen to your plants if, because you were so worried about the possibilities of weeds, you kept digging up the dirt around them? They would die. The same thing happens when we constantly worry about our sins and past regrets. Like Lana's nightmares or Dave's ruminations, these worries about what we have already done or about what has happened to us brings little healing. Worrying about what was already done didn't bring any growth. They needed to leave the past alone and take care of the one thing they had control of: the moment they were actually in.

Some might also ask, *So does living in the now mean we don't make plans for the future?* Absolutely not! If we decided to go on vacation this next summer, the most important time to make that happen is now. We start saving now, we look for flights now, we learn about travel guidelines now. Once we have made a decision that affects the future, the most important time is now. We cannot control the future, but we can be at peace with the future through each choice we make now.

For example, if my child chooses to do his homework today, he increases the odds that he will do his homework again tomorrow, and if he does his homework two days in a row, the chance of him doing homework the third day increases even higher. To be clear, my child doing his homework today doesn't guarantee he will do it tomorrow, but it does increase the probability. So, if we want to affect the future in a positive way, the best place to do that is now.

Christ's commandment to His Apostles is a commandment for us too. "Consider the lilies of the field, how they grow; they toil not, neither do they spin. . . . Wherefore, if God so clothe the grass of the field, which today is and tomorrow is cast into the oven, shall he not much more clothe you. . . . Take therefore no thought for the morrow: for the morrow shall take thought for the things of itself" (Matthew 6:28, 30, 34). God is promising us that if we give our lives to Him, we will have enough. Our worrying doesn't manifest secure futures. Faith in God does.

If we are to live as our Heavenly Father intended us to, we need to exercise faith in Christ and His Atonement now.

What IS the Atonement? The Egg Analogy

Letting go of our pasts and futures, ceding control to our Redeemer, is easier said than done, and the rest of this book will teach you specific thought patterns and behaviors that will help you do that. But before we can jump into those, we must understand what the Atonement really is.

As a child I sometimes watched my mom make eggnog. This was an involved process that entailed separating egg after egg. I was fascinated at how she could deftly crack an egg and then slowly sift the egg back and forth from shell to shell until, in a single, surprising moment, the white would slip from the yolk. It was almost like magic. One moment there was a whole egg being run between her two hands, and then in the next she had the white in one half of the shell and the yolk in the other.

We can think of how Christ's Atonement works in our lives in a similar way. Often in life we commit a sin or mistake and believe we are stuck juggling something rather slippery back and forth, emotionally burdened with guilt and shame. In many ways we have no idea how we can ever be free from the pain that we brought on ourselves or was inflicted on us by the actions of others. We see the mistake and the pain of that mistake as one single entity, like an egg and its yolk. Christ, however, has the ability to separate the pain and shame from the learning and growth that can come out of the mistake. Just like the sifting of the egg, He can help us separate the part of the experience we do need and want from the part that is not what we need and want.

Essentially, Christ makes this offer to us, "I will take the pain, the guilt, the heartache, the suffering—all of it—and leave you with the learning, the growth, the insights, and hope if you will have faith in my Atonement *now*." This process isn't something we as mortals can readily understand. To our understanding it's a bit like me as a child watching my mother separate the eggs. We can watch and watch, but exactly how one part gets pulled from the other is always somewhat inexplicable.

A New Paradigm of Repentance

One day when I was using the egg example in a session with a client, who was quick and bright and very much like Carolyn, she responded, "That makes no sense. Sin and shame are bad things. They separate us from God. They keep us from progressing. But all the parts of an egg are useable. Why would you want to throw them out? In your example it makes it sound like there's no place for repentance."

See? I told you she was bright! This woman hit on a real and troubling misconception of most members of the Church: that repentance is a bad thing. It is a somewhat unsavory process to be used quickly to wipe away the blemishes on our past. Much like a serving of castor oil, it's something we believe we must do to be healthy, but it isn't something we could ever enjoy.

That, however, is not how our Father in Heaven or our Savior see it. Repentance, they've told us repeatedly, is a gift. It's like an egg. At first glance it may seem sticky and hard to handle, but once we've learned how to sift through our experiences, how to use them with all their accompanying emotions, we will have one of God's most useful creations.

We typically think of repentance as a four-part process. We learn this in Primary, and we think of the following four steps that all start with the letter R: recognize, remorse, restitution, resolve. The four Rs you learned might be slightly different, but the process is the same. You must first recognize that you sin. Then you feel remorse that you sinned at all. Next you make restitution for the sin. Finally you resolve to never make the mistake again. That's as easy to understand as a recipe for scrambled eggs.

However, this is actually the simplified version of repentance. It is great for beginning learning in the Primary years and for the relatively simple sins and mistakes we make then. As we mature, though, our understanding of repentance should mature too. Just like you might eat scrambled eggs as a kid but you also appreciate a great soufflé as an adult, your understanding of repentance needs to become something that grows with you.

This is why so many of our leaders have repeatedly implored us to make Christ's Atonement a part of our everyday lives, *part of our now.* This message was repeated both in ancient times and today. In the Book of Mormon, Alma declared, "This life is the time for men to prepare to meet God" (Alma 34:32).

Likewise, in 2012, Elder Bednar posited:

> I suspect that many Church members are much more familiar with the nature of the redeeming and cleansing power of the Atonement than they are with the strengthening and enabling power. It is one thing to know that Jesus Christ came to earth to *die* for us—that is fundamental and foundational to the doctrine of Christ. But we also need to appreciate that the Lord desires, through His Atonement and by the power of the Holy Ghost, to *live* in us—not only to direct us but also to empower us.
>
> . . . Most of us clearly understand that the Atonement is for sinners. I am not so sure, however, that we know and understand that the Atonement is also for saints—for good men and women who are obedient, worthy, and conscientious and who are striving to become better and serve more faithfully. We may mistakenly believe we must make the journey from good to better and become a saint all by ourselves, through sheer grit, willpower, and discipline, and with our obviously limited capacities.[2]

Over and over, our loving Heavenly Father's servants have sought to show us that our Savior's offering is meant to be a part of our everyday lives, not just a ripcord to be pulled when we find ourselves in a freefall of sin. At its roots repentance means, "to feel such a regret for sin that an amendment of life is produced." Repentance, the essence of the Atonement of Jesus Christ, is meant to bring about an amendment to our lives, not an erasure or an obliteration. The Atonement was meant to be simultaneously retroactive and proactive. It applies equally to our pasts and our futures, and in so doing it frees us to live actively in the present moment.

A Newness of Life through a NOW-ness of Life

One day, upon returning home from church, my wife quipped, "Have you ever gone to church and felt inspired, then overwhelmed, and then depressed?" We've all felt this way, right? First, we feel inspired about living our life in a new way, and then we see the gap between where we are and where we want to be, and we feel overwhelmed. Finally, realizing the amount of work it will take to accomplish our desire, we feel depressed, and the *now* is abandoned.

It doesn't have to be that way though. The most beautiful thing about now is that you just need to be present, nothing more. *Now* does not mean you have to figure everything out; it simply asks you to be a part of it. We often forget how powerful we become by letting go and turning our life over to Christ. We don't gain the power to control (something we were never going to have anyway), but we do gain the power to be at peace and present with ourselves, our God, and the universe *now* through surrendering our regrets and anxieties to Christ.

So what does it take to be present in your own life?

In the following chapters, I will explore how you can reclaim your *now*:

- **By being present without judgment**: This step of growth in our lives is critical so that we are not sidetracked from the now by judging others or ourselves. We cannot be in the now and exercise unrighteous judgment at the same time.
- **By being aware of the voice in our head:** We need to develop the ability to put the voice in our head in timeout and ultimately train the voice to be our ally not our enemy.
- **By being aware of our own self-deceptions** (Finding your truest identity): This allows us to be transparent with ourselves, with others, and with God. Through transparency we are finally able to know where we are and who we are.
- **By being still and breathing**: Too often we miss the whisperings

of our Father because our fear-driven primal brain is running the show, and we are unable to just be still, breathe, and listen.

- **By being fearless**: Opportunity often waits for us beyond a veil of fear. We must push through those veils if we are to continue to grow our faith. Growth is not about success or failure but about our willingness to learn and apply.
- **By being connected**: Through our relationships, we will learn to love and be loved. We can learn to be vulnerable and safe with each other thus satisfying our deepest human needs.
- **By being empowered through creation**: As we create beauty we become one with our Creator. We must learn to unify our heart, head, and hands in the creation of beauty and light so that we can draw closer to God now.

Without *now*, we cannot be replenished through our actions or reactions. Nor can we create the new good memories that will continue to exist with us throughout the eternities. Without now, we are unable to love or be loved. Without now, we cannot exercise faith in the things we believe in. Without now, it is impossible to forgive or be forgiven. Without now, our anxieties and regrets will ultimately define us. Without now, we are powerless.

The minute you start to reclaim your now, your life will start to change. You will start to anticipate and look forward to tomorrow and what it will bring. You will also begin to treasure yesterday as it is filled with memories of growing, and the feeling that we are connected to something hopeful. You will finally understand what the Savior meant when He said, "My yoke is easy and my burden is light" (Matthew 11:30).

Notes

1. Neal A. Maxwell, "Remember How Merciful the Lord Hath Been," *Ensign*, May 2004.
2. David A. Bednar, "The Atonement and the Journey of Mortality," *Ensign*, April 2012.

Chapter 6

Be Present without Judgment; Don't Get Sidelined

Lana saw her bishop often, especially after she lost her temple recommend. She was anxious to repent or, as she put it, "Get all this over with." She knew that having sex with the man she was dating was a huge mistake, and of her own accord she went to her bishop and confessed.

At first the repentance process was exhilarating. After each visit she felt hopeful and renewed, and the darkness inside her started to dissipate. Lana brought in the item she was cutting with and asked me to keep it for her so she couldn't hurt herself any more. There was some light coming back to her eyes.

It wasn't a straight shot to healing, though. Repentance was hard. Lana's bishop gave her The Miracle of Forgiveness *to read, and she was struggling to get through it. It was just too intense for her. The pressures of life as a single mom didn't decrease either. She was aware of the Lord's blessings and how He was trying to support her, but she still ended every day in a puddle of exhaustion and anxiety.*

After about six weeks of meeting with her bishop, she said to me, "I thought I'd be done by now. He says I'm not though. When I ask why he says that we'll both know when I'm done and that it's really up to me. Then he asked if I felt I was ready to have my recommend back."

"What did you say?"

"I couldn't answer."

"You said nothing?"

"Yeah. I mean, James, what exactly is keeping me from not screwing up again? What if I sleep with the next guy I date? I mean, I know what I did was wrong, but really it doesn't matter anymore. What's done is done. I'm a licked cupcake. A nailed board. A brownie with a bite out of it. I was before I met Jared. Look at everything I've been through. A troubled childhood? Check. An abusive marriage? Check. Now I've committed fornication. Maybe it doesn't matter if I ever get my recommend back."

I raised my eyebrows. "Do you want it back? Do you want to live in such a way that you can have it back?" I prompted.

"I'm still cutting. Like, I'm trying not to but I still do it. I still swear a lot too. And, honestly, some days I think that if I could find someone like Jared, someone who'd be nice to me, but also wants to stay, that'd be good. I could be happy that way. Maybe this is as good as it gets for someone like me."

" 'Someone like me?' What does that mean?"

"I'm a screw-up, James. Damaged goods."

"Abused but not damaged."

"What difference does that make?"

"What does your bishop say when you tell him you're damaged?"

"He reads me Ether 12:27. I hate that scripture. I hate it so much. I'm so tired of hearing it."

"You don't want to hear about weak things being made strong? Why?"

"I just don't. I mean, maybe that's true for other people, but I've fallen so far. It's just too much."

"What about Christ's Atonement?"

"What about it? That's all the bishop has been talking about. I know all the answers, James. I know that He loves me. I know that He died for me. I know He felt the pain of all my sins. But . . ."

"But what?"

"Something's missing. It isn't working. I still feel weak. Dirty. Lost. A letdown. Damaged." Lana began to cry. "There are some things you just don't bounce back from. You just don't."

"Lana, you're judging yourself much too harshly."

"You're some sort of judgment expert now too, James? You just don't get it."

"No, Lana, you don't get it. The Atonement is not about your judgment; it's about Christ's. You need to stop trying to do His job for Him."

For once, Lana didn't have a ready answer. She was ready to learn.

Dave wasn't about to let himself off easy. His marriage had disintegrated, even though Julie hadn't technically filed for divorce yet. There was no talking to her about anything except the kids. She was smart, and she was decisive. From Dave's description to me, she was a real force to be reckoned with.

"James, I know it seems ridiculous now, but even though she's kicked me out and won't talk to me, it's easier to remember why I married her in the first place. She's strong. She's not the kind of woman to be stopped." Dave shook his head and let out a low whistle. "I don't know how I'm going to change her mind. I don't think I stand a chance. And, really, why should I? Look at me."

Our sessions were starting to feel like a bit of a merry-go-round. Dave would come in and talk about all the things he had lost and how he deserved it. I would try to point out some alternative ways to view things. Dave would argue them down and come to the same conclusion: he screwed up, so he was bad and therefore deserved bad things.

I decided to take a different tactic this time.

"You're right, Dave. I mean, let's look at you. Honestly and truly, why would Julie ever want to be with you? And your kids. Why would they love you? Clearly you're not worth their time or affection. You might as well just give up. Go back to looking at porn. In fact, you might as well just give your life up to it. That's all you're good for anyway, right? Might as well just quit your job and lock yourself in with your computer."

He was stunned for a minute. After looking me up and down for minute he clenched his fists and unclenched them. Dave was vacillating between anger and giving up. It wasn't a direction I usually went in therapy, but I felt like I needed to make Dave angry that day. So I did.

"What's wrong, Dave? You look pretty angry right now. You don't think I should talk to you that way? Why? You've already told me you deserve it."

Dave stood up like he was ready to leave the office.

"Why are you so angry, Dave? Because of how I talked to you?"

He sat down. Then stood up again. He looked me in the eye and took two steps toward the door. He was coming to a moment of decision, and I was pretty hopeful that he would make the decision he did.

"You . . ." he started. "You have no right to talk to me that way."

"Are you sure? After all, this is how you talk to yourself, Dave. Why shouldn't I talk to you that way too?"

"You're my therapist."

"So? What does that mean?"

"Well, for starters it means that you are supposed to be helping me. How does talking like that help me? I'm supposed to come and pay you almost $100 an hour just so you can tell me that I'm garbage?"

"Dave," this time I looked him in the eye, "I haven't said anything you haven't already said about yourself. Why is it okay for you to talk about yourself that way but not me?"

Understanding dawned across Dave's face. He sat back down, and his brow softened as his eyes opened wider. He dropped his shoulders and unclenched his fists.

"You think I'm being too hard on myself."

"Yes, Dave, I do."

"But, James, I've seen so many horrible things. I invited those things into my home and let it skew the way I saw my wife and kids. Sometimes, more times than I ever let on, the images and sounds just come back, and as much as I don't like it., there's a part of me that does. James, I don't think that part is ever going to go away. The carnal man has won. I sold my birthright for a mess of, what do the scriptures call it? Pottage?"

"That's where you're wrong. You haven't sold your birthright. You're only just now coming to understand it. But, Dave, if you've already judged yourself, if you've already decided that you aren't any good or worth investing in, then why are you spending the money to see me? Why are you still hoping that Julie and the kids will come around?"

Dave put his head in his hands and didn't say anything for a while.

Finally he answered, "Because the jury might be out on me, but it isn't out on my kids. There's still hope for them. And as long as I'm screwing up, they don't stand a chance."

"That's noble and commendable. But, Dave, is that all? Is that the only reason you come?"

He stared out the window and answered in a faraway voice. "No. I think . . ." He stopped and took a shaky breath. "I think I'm hoping I'm wrong."

I sat quietly for a moment and then replied, chuckling slightly, "Don't worry, Dave. You are. You're incredibly wrong. You've never been more wrong in your life."

Dave again sat, stunned at my words, but this time he heard me and started chuckling too. "Let's hope so, James. Let's hope so."

A Primer on Being Present

One of the biggest problems of letting your past regrets and future anxieties run your life is that you become perpetually distracted. No matter how engaging the task at hand is, if you are being haunted by your (usually distorted) past or misled by your (perceived) future, you will never actually be in the *now* space. To fix that, the first thing you have to do is learn to be present right here, right now. Or, as President Monson said, "My brothers and sisters, there is no tomorrow to remember if we don't do something today."[1]

Most of us are not very familiar with the idea of being present. Perhaps you've read about "mindfulness" in magazines or heard a podcast about it. Maybe you relate it to some sort of zen practice that somehow resembles yoga or meditation. Those are all good things but not exactly what I mean when I say *presence.*

Presence, in its simplest definition, is the idea of being focused on what you are doing when you are doing it, of making sure your awareness is focused on the moment you are in. It isn't necessarily doing anything different than you are already doing, but it does mean that you think differently about what you are doing. For example, if you are present when you walk outside, you will notice the color of the sky, the smell of the air, the sounds of your neighborhood, the feel of your jacket as you zip it up. Presence is most often found by being aware of our bodily sensations. After all, your mind can wander to the past and the future, but your body can't.

Many Latter-day Saints experience the value of being in the present when they are on their missions or otherwise deeply engaged in service. Think about the last time you were fully immersed in serving someone else. Were you worrying about that mistake you made last week in Sunday School? Were you anxious that your next lesson wouldn't go well? Probably not. Instead you were focused on the tasks at hand. You probably had a clarity and a lightness that you don't usually experience in your everyday life. That's presence.

When we are present in the now, we open up ourselves to our physical senses, the people around us, and to our Heavenly Father's influence. When we can focus on what we are doing, moment to moment, without being drawn into our pasts or our futures, our hearts and minds settle, and it is then that we are most likely to hear the whisperings of the Holy Ghost.

Sounds easy, right?

Unfortunately most of us have one big stumbling block when it comes to being present in our nows.

The Judgment of a Fixed Mind-Set

One reason we often don't stay in the present is that we find it unbearable. This usually happens for one simple reason: judgment. Whether we realize it or not, most of us are usually our own harshest critics. How often do we start a project only to find ourselves remembering that the last time we tried it, it went badly? How often do we sit down with our kids to do homework and worry about how their current grades will affect their futures instead of worrying about how they are doing right now? Those are all judging thoughts. We are judging our pasts and our futures and crowding out our now space so tightly with criticisms that we literally end up feeling squeezed.

Self-recrimination and judgment are possibly the biggest problems that not only land people in my office but also lead them to sin. After all, if we always remembered and believed our true identities as children of the most-high God who loves us and is always willing to help us do better, our mistakes wouldn't be failures. They would be learning opportunities. However, most of us forget who we really are and what God really wants for us and find ourselves stuck. We get mired down in regret for the mistake and the fear that we'll make it again in the future. We judge ourselves as "failures," and this stops us from moving forward. Psychologists have come to call this mind-set a *fixed mind-set* and have found that it poses real dangers when it comes to mental and emotional wellbeing.

This is a dangerous place to be spiritually too. We hear a lot about judgment in the scriptures. Probably the most famous scripture is Christ's injunction that we "judge not, that ye be not judged; yet judge a righteous judgment" (Joseph Smith Translation, Matthew 7:1). This small verse often puts many of us on thorny logical paths that tend to lead in circles. We are not supposed to judge others; that's clear. But we also aren't supposed to not judge everything. After all, God gave us agency, Christ died for our agency, and we have to use that agency to make decisions in order to return to live with our Father in Heaven. Which is, we theorize, where that righteous judgment piece comes in. We can judge just so long as we do it righteously.

Of course, the minute we start to do that, the struggle begins. God's laws are supremely just. They are also supremely impossible to keep perfectly for all of us regular mortals. There's only one person who could do it, and it wasn't you, and it wasn't me. Jesus Christ was the only mortal to ever be able to walk this earth error free, and that was because He was the Son of God. You and I? We are destined for error, mistakes, sins, and failings.

This is the exact problem that Adam and Eve ran into in the Garden of Eden. They were given a set of impossible circumstances within which they had to make a choice. They had to multiply and replenish the earth by having children, but the only way they could do that was by eating the fruit of the Tree of Knowledge of Good and Evil, which they had been commanded not to do. But if they kept that commandment, they would not be able to keep the first commandment to have seed. Either way they would be breaking a commandment. They would be failing—which is what they eventually did. They too were destined for errors, mistakes, sins, and failings. Judgment was swift and resolute. They were cast out of the garden and told that only by hard work would they be able to progress.

Now, if Adam and Eve had fallen prey to a judgment-oriented mind-set, a fixed mind-set, they might have sounded very much like Dave and Lana. "Oh, we screwed up really bad! We were kicked out of the garden! What if our Heavenly Father holds this against us forever? This world is so terrible, but we deserve this. We screwed up, so we are screwups. There's no hope." They could have said all those things, and maybe during some dark moments they did. But scripture tells us that the bigger lesson they learned, faith in God, was greater than the perils of their own fallen natures.

The Mercy of a Growth Mind-Set

When Adam and Eve left the garden, they had a choice: wallow in their sins and mistakes and pine after all that they had lost or simply move forward. Even as He ushered them out of paradise, Heavenly Father reminded them of two all-important factors: a Savior would be provided, and Father would keep answering their prayers.

Sometime after exiting the garden they built an altar and prayed, seeking guidance. Scripture tells us, "And in that day the Holy Ghost fell upon Adam [saying] . . . as thou hast fallen thou mayest be redeemed, and all mankind, even as many as will. And in that day Adam blessed God and was filled, and began to prophesy saying . . . Blessed be the name of God, for because of my transgression my eyes are opened, and in this life I shall have joy." Eve, also inspired, expounded on Adam's feelings, saying, "Were it not for our transgression we never should have seed, and never should have known good and evil, and the joy of our redemption, and the eternal life which God giveth unto all the obedient" (Moses 5:9–11).

Adam and Eve could have chosen the perspective that they had screwed up, and so they deserved the difficulties they were currently having. They could have gotten angry at God and blamed Him for their problems, or they could have rationalized their behavior, thinking, "See? God is unjust. He set us up to fail. This isn't fair." They could've played the victim and blamed Satan, claiming that it wasn't their fault they were in a difficult situation. They could have gotten angry at each other and blamed their hardships on the other person's failing. All of those would have been understandable reactions, and they are ones we ourselves probably have from time to time. These are also all deeply judgmental reactions.

It is significant that Adam and Eve chose something different, something better. They chose to see the good things that came out of their struggle. They chose to see how they could learn. They chose to see how God's love was made manifest in their mistakes. They didn't see themselves as set up to fail. They saw themselves as set up to be redeemed. Instead of embracing a false judgment about themselves, they chose to listen to God and believe in the Atonement and remember what is at its heart: mercy.

It is because they chose that perspective that they were able to embrace what psychologists today call a *growth mind-set*. The growth mind-set is the opposite of the fixed mind-set. Where a fixed mind-set says, "This is the way things are. I can't do this," a growth mind-set says, "This is the way things are right now. I can't do this yet." It's a subtle difference but an important one because it leaves the door open for the reason God sent us all to this earth in the first place: growth and learning. The pattern is clear: our own judgments bring us to a standstill, but God's loving judgment coupled with mercy brings us to growth.

The Ins and Outs of Avoiding Judgment

As pointed out before, fallen, mortal judgment stands in opposition to presence in the now. When we are in a moment and we fill it with judgment, we are automatically falling into the traps of past regrets and future anxieties. Whether aimed primarily at ourselves or those around us, our digressions into the past and future are judgments that we are not qualified to make.

We think most often about outward judgment, about how we are treating other people, but often these outwards judgments are simply projections of inward judgments. The harsher we are with ourselves, the harsher we are with those around us. This turns into a vicious cycle because the more we judge the people around us, the harder we end up judging ourselves. God has been clear about His feelings when it comes to us being judgmental. In the Doctrine and Covenants we are told, "I, the Lord, will forgive whom I will forgive, but of you it is required to forgive all men. And ye ought to say in your hearts—let God judge between me and thee" (Doctrine and Covenants 64:10-11). The old conundrum between not judging and judging a righteous judgment, both ourselves and others, is solved for us by God's omniscience and eternal mercy. Though we may pass judgment on another, the requirement to forgive is not removed. Even if our judgment is completely accurate, we are still required to forgive that person. Maybe one of the reasons God cautions us about judging is because this can create the obstacle in our heart that keeps us from forgiving.

Over the years, I've found three mental habits that help solve both the inward and outward problems of judging. 1) Become a contributor before you become an editor, 2) Avoid spiritual identity theft by embracing eternal identities—both yours and others', and 3) Adopt a paradigm of Heavenly Mathematics (the value of one is equal to the value of all).

Be a Contributor before You're an Editor

A great way to practice being present without judgment is to trade out your usual inner monologue for that of a journalist or contributor to a newspaper. If you were just observing the situation, what would you say about it? You might be tempted to create hyperbolic headlines ("Insane Mother Blows Her Top while Children Run Amok!"), but that's not being a contributor. Instead, if you were actually writing the article, you would write what you notice: toys all over the floor, a mother who has asked fifteen or sixteen times for the kids to stop throwing tennis balls up and down the stairs, and children laughing so loudly they can't (won't?) stop, and the mother getting louder as a result. See the difference? The headline is a judgment. The observations are not.

This works extremely well when it comes to giving up judging yourself, but it also works well with giving up judging others. At my home we have an agreement that you have to be a contributor before you can start editing yourself or someone else. Yes, we actually phrase it that way.

The rule came from my daughter. One night she was telling me about an idea she had. Before she could even finish what she was saying, I started editing her. I told her why it wouldn't work, that it would cost too much, that the logistics would be too complicated. Gently but firmly my daughter looked at me and said, "Dad, you're editing me." With that comment I became aware that I was not being present. I was getting caught up in the past (all the ways I had seen these things not work before) and swept away by the future (it would cost too much and be too complicated). Before my daughter could even finish what she was saying, I had already judged her idea and decided it wasn't good enough.

I took a deep breath, smiled, looked at my daughter, and said, "I'm sorry. Can you start over so I can listen and contribute to what you are saying?" I was now ready to be present without judgment. If we cast judgment on another person, we run the risk of not being able to hear them, love them, or support them. There is always time to edit after we have contributed.

Avoid Spiritual Identity Theft by Embracing Spiritual Identities

Another way judgment takes us away from being present is that it is simply easier. Finding flaws in ourselves and one another is not difficult. In truth, we are all amateurs on this earth, and finding faults is possibly one of the easiest jobs we could ever do. It is also one of the most destructive. For many, finding flaws in others is a favorite pastime. This is not right. Not even God is willing to pass final judgment on us until after this earth life, then the spirit world, and then the millennium is over, yet we are happy to judge ourselves and each other now and harshly.

In some ways, this is a form of identity theft. Just like when someone steals your credit card number and goes on a spending spree, depleting your bank account and stealing your hard-earned money, when we criticize and condemn ourselves or each other with harsh judgments, we take God's work and steal it, using it for our own purposes. Think about it. We are children of the King of heaven. He has invested all of His energy and love and wisdom in bringing about our immortality and eternal life. But when we look in the mirror and decide we are too fat or too stupid or too unlovable, we have confirmed Satan's view of our value and rejected God and His love.

When I was teaching seminary, I had a lesson where I handed out slips of paper to each of my students. On the paper was written a sentence that went something like this, "Did you see that girl with that nasty bathing suit on?" and "Did you see that guy with those gross tattoos?" I then asked the kids to move one word in the sentence so that instead of judging the behavior, they were judging the person. In the first example, they moved the word *nasty*. "Did you see that nasty girl with that bathing suit on?" and in the second example they moved the word *gross*. "Did you see that gross guy with those tattoos?" By moving one word, we are now judging the entire person, and our ability to love or have empathy for them has been lost. Instead of loving, caring, and sharing with our fellow man, we are focusing our energies on judging others and justifying our views.

The key to giving up judgment is to trade your identity back—ask God to show you who you really are. Every human that has lived on this planet has felt worthless at one time or another. Sometimes those feelings are not just for a moment but also permeate every day that we live. So, how do we rise above the feelings of worthlessness that we place on ourselves through self-judgment and find a new image of ourselves?

One way, and possibly the best way, is to ask Father in Heaven, "Can I see me the way You see me? Can I see me through Your eyes?" For too long we have looked at ourselves in a distorted mirror that reflects a warped and twisted view of ourselves. Over time we have come to believe that reflection and accept its image. What we fail to realize is that the mirror we are looking in was constructed by the distortions of a fallen world, not by our Father in Heaven. His mirror reflects all of the hope and potential He sees in us as well as the love He has for us even though we are not perfect. If we are to understand God's love for us, we must be willing to smash the distorted mirror we have been looking in and petition God to let us see ourselves through His eyes, to know ourselves as He know us.

When that prayer is answered, it might be the first time you see yourself as a son or daughter of God and feel the liberation of that knowledge. It is exhilarating to see a small slice of the glory that your Father has planted in you!

Of course, with all knowledge comes responsibility. Once we begin to see who we truly are, we have to stop living below our privileges. We must accept His valuation of us as our own. This is not arrogance; this is simple truth that can liberate us from the self-judgment that has limited our abilities for so long.

Remember Heavenly Mathematics

A huge component to understanding how God sees us is what I like to refer to as *Heavenly Mathematics*. It's a simple formula designed to show you exactly how much you are worth to God. It goes like this: The value of one is equal to all; the value of all is equal to one.

Put another way: You are as valuable to God as the rest of His creations combined; the rest of His creations are just as valuable to God as you are.

Let that sink in for just a moment. God has proclaimed that we are equal in value to all the things He has ever created and that all the things He has ever created are equal in value to us. What an awesome proclamation! Since He is infinite and His creations are infinite, our personal value to Him as His children is infinite. This is what Jesus was trying to explain when He told the parable of the lost sheep. "What man of you, having an hundred sheep, if he lose one of them, doth not leave the ninety and nine in the wilderness, and go after that which is lost, until he find it? And when he hath found it, he layeth it on his shoulders, rejoicing. And when he cometh home, he calleth together his friends and neighbours, saying unto them, Rejoice with me; for I have found my sheep which was lost" (Matthew 15:4-6).

In some ways this parable doesn't make sense. After all, it's just one sheep. Why is it worth searching for the one when you have ninety-nine others?

Because, as a shepherd, you know that sheep and value it. It isn't just about the flock as a whole. It's about the individual sheep too. The value of the flock depends in part on the value of the individual sheep. And because the shepherd knows the sheep, the value of the one sheep is equal to the value of the herd.

It is the same with us and the Good Shepherd. Because one is equal in value to all, He seeks out the one that is lost. Thus, God does not see us in terms of acceptable loss but is compelled to seek us out individually and collectively. We may often find ourselves devaluing ourselves, believing we are worthless or broken. However, if God has proclaimed our value to be equal to all things He has ever created, who are we to argue?

Judgment Is the Opposite of Love

I'll reiterate this fact one more time: we are valuable to God in such an astounding way because He loves us. This is how His judgment and His mercy can always work together for our good. But mortal judgment, our judgment, is the opposite of love, and when we do it we lose access to now and the ability to love and be loved. Let me offer a sort of parable of my own to explain.

Once, while I was at a restaurant with my family, a young man walked in with a friend. On the young man's shirt were two hands. One hand had its middle finger sticking up, and the other hand was pointing outward toward whoever was looking at the shirt. As the young man and his friend were being escorted by the hostess, I kept thinking in my mind, *don't sit them by us, please don't sit them by us*. As if my thoughts were a magnet, she sat them directly across from my family where my kids could see the young man's shirt.

As we ate our dinner, I found myself becoming agitated. I thought, "What gives that kid the right to say such a thing to my family?" As our meal got near to being over, a plan formed in my head. I decided I would walk with my family to the car and then tell my wife I had forgotten my keys and go back into the restaurant and have a word (not a kind word) with the young man.

As we were getting ready to leave, something incredible happened; a pure thought formed in my mind and burned in my heart. With great resistance I tried to push the thought out, but I knew where it had come from. As the waitress came to our table to give us our check, I asked her if she would do me a favor. She said yes. I pointed to the two young men sitting by our table and told her I was buying their dinner that night.

There have been a few times in my life that I have felt great peace come over me, and this was one of them. By listening to the Spirit and choosing love over judgment, I was able to see this young man as a son of

God. In that moment I came to understand that good really is stronger than evil and that Christ's love for us, and our love for each other, really can conquer all. I could see how his individual value was equal to the value of everyone in God's eyes.

As we got up to leave, the young man, understanding what had just happened, looked at me and said, "No one has ever done anything like that for me before. Thank you."

My heart filled. Before I listened to the Spirit I was absolutely caught up in editing that young man. I was also aiding in the spiritual identity theft he had committed against himself. And I had completely forgotten the importance of Heavenly Mathematics. Obviously, by wearing a shirt like that, he was showing that he didn't understand his true identity as a son of God. My anger at him was a judgment that hinged on me being better than him and denying his value. But then God opened my eyes. Love opened up a door that judgment could not.

It is the same for each of us. Whether we are judging others or ourselves, that judgment will be fallible. No matter how careful we are or how right we believe ourselves to be, our own judgments will always be incorrect. The only judgment we can trust is God's judgment—and that is always grounded in love. His love, as verified by Christ's Atonement, is there to free you from judgment so you can simply be here now.

Note

1. Thomas S. Monson, "Finding Joy in the Journey," *Ensign*, November 2008, 85.

Chapter 7
Turn Down the Voices in Your Head

Carolyn was, like usual, worried.

This time, though, it wasn't just about the kids or her husband or her bank account and her bills or her calling or the cleanliness of her house. This time she was worried about herself.

"James, something's really wrong. I mean, really. With me. The other day I woke up and I couldn't stop freaking out. It started before breakfast. The kids weren't even up yet, and I was already coming up with the things I was going to do wrong. I was barely out of bed and I already knew the ways in which I was going to fail. I'm getting worse. Something is really wrong."

"That makes you pretty much like the rest of world then, Carolyn. But I think you've been saying that for a while now. What do I usually say to that?"

She was momentarily stumped. "Well, usually you make me lay out exactly what I'm worried about, and as I'm talking I see that they are sort of silly." She blushed and looked down at her hands in her lap.

"I wouldn't say silly," I interjected, "but maybe a bit distorted. Have we talked about distorted thinking?"

"No, but I've read about it. It's when your thought patterns don't always, well, work right, I guess."

"Right. Usually we think that our thoughts, the voices in our heads, are telling us the whole story, giving us an unvarnished picture. We think of them like mirrors for reality. But, really, our thoughts are more like funhouse mirrors than true reflections."

Carolyn pursed her lips as she thought this over. "So, what you're saying is that when I worry, I'm lying to myself. I really am messed up!"

"Slow down. That's not exactly what I'm saying. Think back to the metaphor. A funhouse mirror shows you a reflection of yourself, right?"

"Yes . . ."

"But it doesn't show you exactly how you really look, right? The mirrors show you as either very stretched out or very squished. They make your face twice as big as your torso and your legs shorter than your arms. They distort your image. Our thoughts can do the same thing."

"But, James, it's not like I'm anorexic or something. I mean, I would like to lose ten pounds, and I know that my body isn't that pretty but I don't think I see myself as . . ."

"That's one way our thoughts get distorted, the way we view our bodies. But distorted thinking is actually much more subtle than that. Let's go back to your freak out the other morning, when you were stressing out and coming up with all the ways you could fail before the kids even got out of bed. What were the options for you that day?"

"Huh? Well, I was debating between whether or not I should make the kids pancakes or eggs or both for breakfast. I really didn't want to get the kitchen that dirty, and making both seemed like it would take a lot of time, but I also knew that Katie had a test that day, and I didn't want her getting hungry, so—"

I cut her off. "I don't mean the breakfast options, although that is very kind of you to make breakfast for your kids and to put so much thought and effort into it. Not necessary, but kind of you. I mean big picture. Your options that morning were actually only two things because of how you usually think. You usually set it up so your day can only go one of two ways."

"That makes no sense. I mean, our daily schedule is crazy. There a million ways things can go wrong and I can fail."

"There it is. You've found the first option: failure."

As Carolyn's eyes met mine she looked like a deer in the headlights. "You mean I set things up as either a success or a failure? With no in-between?"

"Yep. It's black-and-white thinking. A very common cognitive distortion. It's like looking in the funhouse mirrors and believing that your body must be the incredibly squished version in one mirror or the entirely stretched-out version in the other mirror. Neither one is real, and both are extreme."

"But, life is about success and failure, isn't it? I mean, you're either getting better each day or you're not. Didn't Joseph Smith say that? There are no fence sitters, right?"

"I don't think Joseph Smith ever actually said that. It's one of those myths we come up against a lot at church. But Jesus Christ did say, 'Come unto me all ye that labor and are heavy laden and I will give you rest.' He also said that we should forgive seventy times seven. He also told a story about laborers who started in the morning being paid the same as those who started in the evening. Doesn't seem to me like a success-or-failure-only model."

"But if that's not how things are, if that's a cognitive distortion, then how I am supposed to think? How do I do that right? Sheesh, even my thoughts are failing me now!"

"Carolyn, you're missing the point. The point is not how you are supposed to do things or that you are failing at one more thing. The point is that you can change how you think, and when you do that, you'll change how you feel."

She sighed, knitting her brow. "Change how you think to change how you feel? That doesn't make much sense, but I guess I'll give it a try."

I couldn't help but smile. "Now we're getting somewhere!"

Since Dave had gotten angry in my office and realized how toxic his own thinking about himself was, I'd given him an assignment to start noticing every time he said something mean to or about himself. His report was not particularly encouraging but was also very typical of my clients.

"James, it's almost like everything I say to myself is negative. Everything I do is bad. It's pretty discouraging."

"Yeah? Did you write down exactly what those thoughts were?"

Dave pulled a paper out of his pocket, unfolded it, and passed it across the table to me. It was fairly standard. Things like, "I always screw up." Or, "You got lucky that time. You usually mess that up." Even the good old, "What did you expect? Why would it be different this time?" covered the page.

"This is pretty bleak," I replied.

"No wonder I'm depressed, right?" Dave laughed ruefully.

"Writing them down was just step one. Now we start rewriting them. After all, your thoughts don't determine reality. YOU do. If you don't like what's in your head, then you get to change it."

"That sounds nice. So if I want to be a millionaire and out of debt, every time I get down on myself for struggling with money I just have to chant 'I'm a millionaire. I'm a millionaire.' Then my money problems disappear!"

We both laughed that time. "You can try that. Let me know if it works. But what I was going to suggest was that you choose one or two thoughts, and when you notice them in your head, rephrase them. For example, instead of saying, 'I always screw up.' Say, 'I screwed up this time, but that's because I'm still learning. How can I do better next time?' How do you think that would work?"

Dave raised his brows and thought for minute. His face looked like he might try to argue with me but he decided to relent instead. "It might work. I mean, it's worth a shot. It sounds kind of cheesy, but as long as I don't have to say it out loud I don't see how it could hurt."

Walking on Water Every Day

One of my favorite scripture stories is the one where Peter walks on water. It's also the one where Peter falls in the water. How you view it depends on whether you're a glass-half-empty or a glass-half-full kind of person. You probably remember it.

This story happens right on the heels of the miracle with five loaves and two fishes. At the beginning of the chapter, Christ's cousin, John the Baptist, is beheaded, and Jesus seeks solace in the desert. He is followed by a multitude, though, and has compassion on them, healing them and ministering to them. As night comes on, the disciples suggest Christ send everyone home, but He has bigger plans. He performs the miracle of feeding the five thousand. Once He knows the multitude is taken care of, Christ sends the disciples on their way across the sea and heads into the mountains for some much-needed solitude.

As the evening progresses, the disciples are still in the boat and a storm sets in. Apparently it's a fairly good storm because it lasts through the night and into the early morning hours. Staring out across the water they see a figure and immediately assume it is a ghost. As their fear sets in, Christ calls out to them saying, "Be of good cheer; it is I; be not afraid" (Matthew 14:27).

Peter, sometimes impetuous but always courageous, calls back, "Lord, if it be thou, bid me come unto thee on the water." Christ does, and Peter climbs out of the boat, making his way on nothing but the waves beneath him.

Now, as if there isn't enough drama going on, Peter begins to be buffeted by the winds swirling around him. He glances away from the Savior and begins to sink, crying out a prayer that is undoubtedly familiar to most of us modern readers, "Lord, save me" (Matthew 14:30).

In that perilous moment, Christ does for Peter what He does for all us. He immediately stretches out His hand, catches him up, and saves him. The Lord then asks Peter a question that He also asks each of us, "O thou of little faith, wherefore didst thou doubt?" (Matthew 14:31).

When Peter was focused on the Lord, he could do the impossible. When he was focused on the storm, he could barely keep himself from drowning. It's the same for each of us—we all know that. So why do we so often forget?

The answer to that question has everything to do with how we think. So often we phrase this as a faith question. As in: Peter was able to walk on water because he had faith, or the Lord reprimanded him for not having faith. But I don't think that's the whole story. I think it is a story about what we believe about ourselves and about God's desire to change that.

Our Thoughts: Headwinds or Tailwinds of Faithfulness?

One of the most powerful tools we have as humans is something we cannot ever see, touch, or even sometimes fathom. It's the power we have to think. It is our amazing cognitive and philosophical abilities that set us apart from all the other mammals roaming the earth. However, it is also one of our biggest liabilities.

An oft-quoted aphorism states it this way, "We sow our thoughts, and we reap our actions; we sow our actions, and we reap our habits; we sow our habits, and we reap our characters; we sow our characters, and we reap our destiny."[1] Our great abilities to think can either take us to great habits and character or to, well, not-so-great habits. We usually think of this in reference to thinking "bad thoughts" leading to sins, but there is a much more pervasive, and perhaps dangerous, way this works.

The way our thoughts influence us starts while we're young. Around the age of two to four years old we discovered language, and this created a new voice inside us. In the beginning the new voice could be heard by everyone around us as we babbled away, "What's that? How come? Why? Where is it?" At first it is cute to our parents as we rambled on, discovering our world through language, but then our parents taught us about being quiet and placed a finger to their lips. We learned to prevent our voice from being externalized, but the voice never stopped talking. It continued narrating in our heads, and it continues to this very day.

In the early years of our life the voice was almost exclusively a voice of discovery. We wanted to know about everything. In time the voice began to change as we were introduced to guilt, shame, secrets, and judgment. It changed shapes as the people and influences around us starting talking in negative ways (sometimes purposefully and some by accident). Instead of being a voice that was seeking to help us understand the world around us and grow, the voice started to become judgmental, cynical, fearful, destructive, and hopeless.

The voice eventually worked like a script in our minds, and it is one we are so accustomed to we often don't even notice it. For many this script is relentlessly negative. That negative script becomes something we simply accept, forgetting that it is nothing more than voice. In an attempt to drown out that voice some turn to shopping, over-exercising, dieting, alcohol, drugs, electronics, self-mutilation, and other distractions.

But what happens when the voices in our head aren't negative? If the negative voices are powerful enough to drive us to things like addiction, would a positive voice be powerful enough to turn our lives in a completely different direction?

The answer to that is an enthusiastic *yes*. Just like Peter walking on the water, it is what we focus on that determines our success. It isn't our circumstances or experiences but rather how we think that makes the impossible possible.

Common Headwinds

The way we think can either work against us, like a headwind against a sailboat, or they can help propel us forward, like a tailwind. Which direction they push us really depends on what kind of thoughts we cultivate. Thoughts that push us back like headwinds are typically called *cognitive distortions*. These are thoughts that seem perfectly reasonable up close but are not actually very reasonable at all when you take a wider view. There are actually a lot of different types of distortions, and very few people will engage in all of them. There are, however, a few types of cognitive distortions that I see often and that many well-meaning LDS folk fall prey to.

Black-and-White Thinking

This type of cognitive distortion is most easily characterized by the way young children think. When kids are little everything is either good or bad, right or wrong. There are no in-betweens or halfways. They either love their dinner or they hate it. Their little brother or sister is their best friend or their worst enemy.

As adults, we can often see the in-betweens when it comes to our dinners or books or movies. Plenty of things are just fine. But we don't always see the in-betweens when it comes to big picture things. How many times have you let one little slip up make you feel like your entire life is a failure? You are either amazing at your job or terrible. You are either the best Sunday School teacher or the worst. You often see the people around you as either good or bad. Choices can only be right or wrong. With this mind-set there is no room for growth or improvement. It's perfection now, or never.

Here's a simple way to figure out if black-and-white thinking is something holding you back. Ask yourself how you feel about a recent family gathering. If you start to focus on the things that went wrong, the things that could have gone better, and the things you feel stupid about, and you begin to categorized the experience as good or bad, you are probably a black-and-white thinker to some degree.

Filtering

Filtering is another extremely common distortion, and it is has more to do with our perceptions than our exact thoughts. Filtering in general is fairly easy to understand. We filter water to get the impurities out, keeping the best parts of the water to drink. Several organs in our bodies work as filters to get the toxins out of our bodies, keeping only the nutrients we need.

When we filter our thoughts it is often the opposite of how we filter other things in our lives. When we filter our thoughts we tend to separate our perceptions into valid or invalid. Often it is our negative thoughts we see as being the most valid. For example, if you make a nice dinner but the casserole is slightly burned and you engage in filtering, then you feel like the most important thing is the casserole being burned. Your mind will focus on that perception and magnify it, all the while minimizing the good things like how much everyone enjoyed the salad and the great conversation. Filtering takes all the good and pushes it out and makes only the bad important.

So, if you think back on your last family get-together and can list ten or twelve negatives for every positive, there's a good chance you are filtering and engaging in distorted thinking.

Heaven Reward Fallacy

In a popular rock song by The Offspring called "Self Esteem," the person in the song says a famous line, "the more you suffer the more it shows you really care."

A couple had been visiting me for about six months. The husband had narcissistic behaviors, and the wife had convinced herself that the more she suffered in the relationship, the more it showed she cared. She would often quote a scripture that would show a single dimension of the Savior's behavior at the exclusion of all His other teachings. She would focus on verses that talked about long suffering, enduring to the end, loving your enemy, forgiving others' trespasses. All of her verses were true teachings, but they were isolated from many other gospel principles that Jesus taught that encourage us to confront evil, address abuses, establish good boundaries, and embrace truth so we can be set free.

Underlying this person's view was the belief that in the next life she would be rewarded for her suffering. Of course if we go a layer deeper, we see a person that was being driven by fear, had become passive due to abuse, and was seeking justification for not being willing to stand up for herself.

Though religion can often be the catalyst for a healthy spiritual, physical, and emotional life, it can also be used to impede progress and give us excuses to continue unhealthy behaviors. In this situation, the person was able to see how she had used gospel principles to blind her from the truth and justify behavior that would continue to invite abuse. Through therapy, both were able to establish the kind of healthy boundaries that allow individuals to flourish in a relationship. We too must be aware when we are selectively using principles of truth in a vacuum to accommodate our current unhealthy behavior assuming God will reward us for our suffering, even though we had the power all along to improve our situation.

If you find yourself identifying with the wife in the story above, you probably engage in this distortion.

The Past-Is-the-Present Fallacy

Through groundbreaking research by Dr. Elizabeth Loftus, an expert on memory creation and distortion, we now understand how memories can become distorted, enhanced, altered, re-created, and falsified. Through her research we have come to understand how distorted memory recall can affect how we act today.

One of my clients that visited regularly would often reference her past experiences, which were usually negative, to establish her emotional state in the present. Extensive amounts of time were being spent reliving past injustices and using those memories to establish how she felt now. Over time, it became apparent that not only were past memories being used to fuel her current anger and irritation, she was also beginning to embellish and enhance certain memories to provide additional justification for her current feelings of despair and vengeance.

At one point it became very clear that some of the details of her memories were inaccurate. When I questioned her about these significant detail discrepancies, she became angry and accused me of calling her a liar and attempted to move away from the topic. When she became aware that I wasn't going to just accept her stories without question, we began to focus on the distortion she had been injecting into her past memories to enhance and expand her anger.

It is difficult to constructively confront someone who is altering and distorting their memories to justify the intense feelings they have now. In this situation, the client had an incredible desire to be seen in the "poor me" light and harvest sympathy from almost anyone who would listen. Though it appeared there was some genuine abuse that had affected this person's life, it was even more obvious that the past was being embellished and distorted to gain sympathy now. In some ways, the quick fix she was receiving from others was sympathy, and this was helping her to numb the pain she was feeling in the present, but it was ultimately having a negative long-term effect.

Because the past was willfully being distorted for short-term gain, it was going to make it impossible for this person to find long-term healing and be made whole through the Savior's Atonement. The Atonement requires us to bring our most honest self to the altar so the Lord can truly heal our wounds and make us whole.

While most will not engage in this to the degree that my client did, many of us do this in small ways. If you find that you often bring up the past to explain your present moment or to predict your future, this distorted pattern might be in your thinking too.

Fallacy of Fairness

Not too many years ago, the Church launched a program called, "I'm a Mormon." In ads on TV and on the internet, a wide variety of members of the Church were presented. In many ways the people we saw in these ads did not fit the typical LDS missionary stereotype: white shirt and tie, short hair, clean shaven, and white.

During a session with a client who often focused on the unfairness of life these ads were brought up. My client, in a frustrated voice, said, "It's not fair." She continued to explain that she had lived her life just as the Church had seemed to ask her to, and now it was glorifying all these people that had no obvious outward emphasis on a "proper Mormon image."

It was interesting to listen to this person talk about all the effort she had made to follow Church standards, and now the Church seemed to be saying that all that effort didn't really matter. As we discussed her situation further, I couldn't help but think of the parable of the eleventh-hour worker and the feeling that others had toward him. They felt it was unfair that they had been working all day for the same price that the person who just entered the field in the eleventh hour would receive.

I discussed this example with my client who had never considered that the person in the parable, complaining in the field, was her. She had become fixated so much on what was fair, she failed to understand the incredible mercy from God that is necessary for all of us to progress.

This distortion is particularly harmful because it cuts us off from receiving the blessings God wants to give us—and the ones He is already giving us—because we can't see them. If you are the type of person who is often envious of others or spends a lot of time thinking about whether things are fair or not, you are probably engaging in this distortion too.

Other cognitive distortions include

- Globalizing (using one experience as the rule for everything else)
- Jumping to conclusions (with little to no evidence, you assume you understand other people's motives and can predict their actions)
- Catastrophizing (assuming the worst will always happen; turning everything into a catastrophe)
- Personalization (making other people's actions and feelings a direct result of your actions; everything is about you personally)
- Control fallacies (the belief that your actions and moods control other people's actions and moods; the belief that you are responsible for the feelings and actions of others)
- Blaming (everyone else is responsible for your life and the problems in it; you are always the victim)
- Shoulds (when most of your thoughts or motivations are because you *should* do something)
- Emotional reasoning (because you feel something, it must be the truth)

Turning Headwinds into Tailwinds

Now, odds are you probably found yourself identifying with one or more of the above cognitive distortions. Don't worry; we all do to one degree or another. That's why we all need to turn down the voices in our heads. They aren't always reliable!

What is important is recognizing that you are engaging in distorted thinking and correcting it when it happens. Gradually over time you will start to engage in distorted thinking less and less often, effectively turning those psychological and emotional headwinds into tailwinds.

There are actually a few really simple tricks you can use to take charge of the voice inside your head that will help eliminate almost all the cognitive distortions you engage in. You don't even need to know exactly which one is pulling your thoughts out of shape at the moment. Using any of the techniques that follow will help.

Become the Journalist of Your Own Experience

A lot of the time clients will mistakenly think that they need to make it so they have absolutely no voices in their heads whatsoever. You'll notice I didn't say that. The way our minds work, we are always narrating our experience. We just want to do it consciously and use it to help us grow. As human beings we have a story to tell, so we might as well tell it right. Some of the greatest storytellers in our world are journalists, and you can take a few cues from them when it comes to managing your inner monologue.

The first rule of journalism is to record, not judge. Some journalists will state their opinion, but great journalists simply observe the facts and set them down on paper. The voice in our head often turns distorted when it works like biased reporters. Instead of looking at all the available evidence, they simply pick the things that support an already flawed viewpoint. That easily turns into black-and-white thinking, catastrophizing, and other distorted thinking patterns. Train your inner voice to be a journalist, not an alarmist.

Look for Opposite Evidence

Another simple straightforward tactic for turning down the voices in your head is to start looking for opposite evidence. One way the voice in your head will work against you is by using what's called a confirmation bias. This means all the voice does is notice things that uphold the viewpoint you already have.

This was something Dave really struggled with. He knew very well that he had messed up and that his wife's feelings were valid. None of that was distorted thinking. In fact, it was good that he was willing to admit his mistakes and how they had affected his family. However, his thinking quickly became distorted because he only let his inner voice think about his mistakes. His inner voice got better and better at finding his mistakes and problems until that was all he saw.

Now, Dave did make some pretty solid mistakes but fixating on them was not helpful. He needed to start to look for ways he could turn his mistakes into opportunities. Looking only at the things he did wrong made it so he had no path forward. If he had started looking at opportunities for growth in his struggles like we were practicing in his personal writing, it would have given him some ideas on how to improve his relationship with his wife and start making amends.

Check the Voice against Your Divine Identity

The truth is that even God doesn't berate us for sinning. He wants us to recognize our sins and find a useful path forward. He will always build you up. He will always give you hope. Your inner voice should do the same.

For many, because their voice has been out of control for so long, they have forgotten who they are and their divine origin. They only hear the voice inside describing them as the world sees them. They have forgotten that God sees our value as unlimited and eternal, and He wants us to view ourselves through His eyes so that we can experience His love and hope for us. He wants us to let His vision of ourselves sink into our hearts so that we will stop listening to the distorted voice and embracing the twisted images of ourselves that Lucifer so delightfully uses against us.

If Jesus were speaking about the voice inside us, He might say, "You were not created to serve the voice, the voice was created to serve you."

Much of the negative fuel for our voice comes from judging. As we judge, we begin to fill our heart with anger, envy, and hate. These strong emotions are often latched onto by our voice, and soon we are hearing a negative tirade in our head that will eventually affect our attitude, our actions, and finally our life. However, we know that we are beings made in the image of a Godly Father who is the source of all light and life. He sent His Son to bring that light and life to the world for each of us, individually. He does not dwell on the negative. He dwells on truth—and so should we.

Walking on Water

If not kept in check, our judgments and lies will fuel a never-ending cycle of us serving our voice and our voice controlling our life. The Apostle James said, "Behold, we put bits in the horses' mouths, that they may obey us; and we turn about their whole body" (James 3:3). We must place a bit in the mouth of our voice that rules our head too.

When we start to direct the voice in our heads we are like Peter when he jumped out of the boat and began walking toward the Savior. It wasn't that the storm had changed but it was that Peter believed he could do what the Savior was asking him to do. He was so focused on the Savior, all doubt had left his mind.

Of course, Peter wasn't perfect, and he did start to notice the storm around him, and that's when he started to sink. The storm was so strong that the wind started to push him back. We don't know, but there's a pretty good chance that Peter had a moment where the voices in his head told him he couldn't do it, he wasn't the Son of God but just a mortal, he shouldn't be able to do what he was doing.

All of us will find ourselves in Peter's place, where God has asked us to do what seems impossible. The voices in our head proclaims all the reasons we can't do it but God's spirit can speak peace to our souls and help us to gather the faith needed to follow His Son. As our feet and hands serve the Lord, the voice in our head can also be unified with our faith so that mountains can be moved, and, perhaps even more magnificent, we can be made whole.

Note

1. Wayne S. Peterson, "Our Actions Determine Our Character," *Ensign*, November 2001, 83–84.

Chapter 8
Be Aware of Self-Deception

Lana was starting to frustrate me. In the beginning of my sessions with her she had been in a dark and sad place. The overwhelming theme of our sessions then was, "Things can't go on this way." And they didn't. She got divorced. She moved. She was doing an excellent job figuring out how to be a strong single mom for her kids. For a while I watched her push through some of the hardest barriers she had faced. But since she had met Jared, all the momentum she had gained started spinning out.

Today, as she sat down in my office she couldn't even bring herself to look me in the eye. She usually started our sessions off with a burst of chatter, but not today.

She was starting to get frustrated with herself too. Not that she'd admit it.

After waiting a few minutes I started, "So, how goes it? It's been a few weeks since we talked. Where're you at these days?"

"Where do you expect me to be at, James? Maybe we should just start there."

"Why? Do you only come to our appointments because of my expectations? This process is about you, Lana."

"Right. Sure. Whatever. How about this? I'll tell you that everything is great, and I'm taking the sacrament again, and I love my job, and my kids are angels, and then we can just be done."

"If you want to waste my time and yours, you can do that. Sure."

"Oh, great. So now I'm wasting your time?" Her tone was acid. It really made me wonder what happened since the last time I saw her.

"Let's take a breath for a minute and try again, Lana."

"I'm bad at breathing. We've been through this, James."

"Fine. I'll breathe, and you can sit there and be upset."

She rolled her eyes in such an exaggerated way it rivaled that of my teenage clients.

I took a couple deep breaths and tried again. "So, you mentioned the sacrament. Are you taking it again?"

"No."

"No?"

"No. I'm not ready yet."

"Really? Why not?"

"Well, I took it once, and it was good, but then, well, I screwed up again, and my bishop told me that if I kept this up he'd have to do a disciplinary council, so I just decided it wasn't worth it. I'll just keep going to church and not take it, and then I can't do any worse."

"That sounds like a terrible idea to me. Why would you put in the effort of going to church but not claim the blessings?"

"Because the blessings come with a price, James. God's grace isn't free, and there's no way I'll ever be able to pay my tab, so I need to stop racking up new charges."

My clients don't often leave me speechless, but I didn't know where to start with Lana. I decided to just go with honesty. "Lana, a while ago you were on the brink of big things. You were finally beginning to understand Christ's Atonement and all it has to offer. But now we're back to things like 'God's grace isn't free.' I don't even know what to say right now. I'm pretty frustrated."

"Welcome to the club."

This time I rolled my eyes.

Lana lit into me, "What do you expect, James? I'm a single mom. I'm barely making ends meet. I'm a victim of sexual abuse. I'm a cutter. I'm a screwup! Why is that so hard for you to understand? This is as good as it gets. I might as well take what I can when I can because that's all there is."

I quieted my voice and responded in a near-whisper, "No. That is false, and you know it is. The first and most powerful lie a liar tells is the one they tell themselves. You've convinced yourself that you're a victim and that's all. Lana, you know there is more to you than that."

"So now I'm a liar too? Thanks a lot, James." Her words were angry, but her tone was defeated.

"Lana, you are not a liar, but you have accepted an incredibly dangerous lie. You've accepted that you are the kind of person things can only happen to, not the kind of person who can take charge of her life. What happened? Why are you accepting that untruth about yourself?"

"I broke up with Jared. But he came back. And now he tells me every time he sees me that this is the last time and that sleeping with me is a huge mistake, and he's never coming back but he still wants to be my friend. Then he doesn't come around or call, until he's lonely or I'm in a rough spot. And then we have sex. It's a mess, and I don't know how to get out. I don't want to do this, but I just keep doing it. Maybe because at least this is better than what I had. Maybe this is as good as it gets. Maybe it's good enough. See? I'm a screwup. I thought the things that happened in my marriage were my all-time low, but this . . . I swore I'd never be in a place that made it so I couldn't look my children in the eye, but here I am." She started crying.

"So, you're letting Jared decide what you're worth. And he's treating you like you're worth nothing."

"It doesn't matter anyway."

"There you go, lying to yourself again. Lana, you matter. Of course you do. No number of mistakes will change your eternal worth. It's time we work on you telling yourself the truth."

Carolyn walked in briskly and sat down, smiling. The teary-eyed, exhausted mom was gone. In her place was a typical Type-A woman. Something about the abrupt turnaround unnerved me.

"You look good today, Carolyn. How have you been since our last session?"

"Great, James. Just great. Things are starting to come together. I've got a handle on things again. I'm thinking that this may be our last session."

"That's excellent. My goal is always to get my clients back out into the world. They are welcome to come back whenever they need, but it's always a great day when we say goodbye. What makes you think you're ready to be done?"

"It all started at my youngest's parent-teacher conference. His teacher had so many good things to say, and I realized something very important: even if I'm feeling stressed and maybe a bit crazy, it doesn't actually matter

because it looks fine on the outside, and it is working. So, why am I over-analyzing this? Why am I coming here? My life is fine. I am fine just the way I am."

I nodded slowly, digesting her words. "Go on."

"Thank you. So, I just decided that I need to work from the outside in. If I get up early every morning and work out, get dressed, and put my makeup on, I'll not just look pulled together, I'll feel pulled together, and then I'll be pulled together. And even if I'm not, it doesn't matter because as long as other people just see things working, then it is *working."*

"You don't see a disconnect in there, Carolyn? What about your kids and husband? This sounds a lot like what you were doing before you started seeing me. Back then you were having panic attacks and trouble sleeping."

"I don't see what this has to do with my kids and husband. They'll just see a pulled together mom, and that's all they want. As for the trouble sleeping, well, I'm sure there's a pill for that."

"If you want to be done with therapy, Carolyn, that's a choice you can make, but I think it might not be the right one. I think with this new plan, you'll be living a lie."

Carolyn was momentarily ruffled but did her best to cover it. "James, I'm not a liar, and I don't think it's fair of you to say that."

"Carolyn, I'm not saying you *are a liar, but I am saying that you will be engaging in a level of deception that will limit you a lot. Not just with your husband and kids but also with God. No matter how pulled together you look on the outside, He knows what is happening in your heart, and, Carolyn, He doesn't want just your actions. He wants your heart. How is this outside-in living going to help you draw closer to Christ?"*

Her shoulders sagged, and the familiar weariness began to creep back in. "I don't want to keep relying on Him like that. I want to show Him that I can do this. I'm going to prove to Him that I get it. I get how much my Heavenly Father loves me so I can move on now, you know? I've learned, and I'm ready to get back in there and do the work."

"So you're going to pay Him back? You're going to make up for Christ's Atonement?"

"Well . . . no. Yes. Maybe. I don't know, James. It just felt so good to be seen as having it all together. I want to go back to that."

"But at what cost, Carolyn? What are you willing to sacrifice in order to keep up appearances?"

Who I Am Is What I Am Is Who I Am

I was told once that in the Middle East one of the greatest compliments you can offer a person is to tell them, "You are the same on the inside as you are on the outside." What an incredible recognition to give to another person. Can you even imagine a person with no pretense, no facade, and no illusion of who they are? Instead of the person spending precious energy to create an image of who they want to be, they are simply themselves. And all the energy that would have been spent creating the illusion is spent loving, caring, sharing, growing, and being one with themselves and God.

Sounds pretty amazing, right? It probably sounds a little impossible too. But it isn't. Over my years of working as a therapist I've seen incredible changes in everyone: teenage sex offenders, stay-at-home suburban moms, highly paid professionals. And they all have one thing in common: letting go of who they think they are and accepting who they truly are.

Aligning the self you present to the world with your inner self is necessary not only for peace and healing, but it's also the only way to let go of your past and stop worrying about your future. After all, if you are worried about how you present yourself instead of being real, you are constantly working to cover your tracks and control others' perceptions. Now *that* sounds pretty impossible.

The Beginnings of Deception

Do you know who the first person was that Lucifer lied to? The father of lies started out well before he ever spoke to Adam or Eve. It was even before he spoke up at the Council in Heaven. He lied first and foremost to himself. Before he could approach Heavenly Father or even hope to convince other spirits to follow him, he had to tell himself that his plan was superior to our Father in Heaven's. As he proceeded to act on this belief, and has continued to act on it ever since, he fell farther and farther away from our Father's and our Savior's influence. Scripture tells us, "He was a murderer from the beginning, and abode not in the truth, because there is no truth in him. When he speaketh a lie, he speaketh of his own: for he is a liar, and the father of it" (John 8:44).

If you stop to think about it, this is how Satan works with us too. Almost every single thing he gets us to do, every sin we commit, actually starts with the same thing: Satan gets us to lie to ourselves. We will all make mistakes and errors, which have nothing to do with Satan, but when it comes to sin it usually starts when we are not honest with ourselves.

It might make you uncomfortable, but if you stop and think about it, you can probably remember a time when you have lied to yourself, started to believe those lies, and then formed your actions around the lie. Usually, we don't call this lying. We call it rationalizing or justifying. For many of us, a lifetime will be spent justifying our lies as truth just as Lucifer does. Instead of working to align our actions with our beliefs and values that are founded in truth, we choose to rewrite our beliefs and values to accommodate our situations.

We do this in big ways sometimes, but more often than not, these are small lies that we tell ourselves. They usually crop up through our inner voice when we are scared or angry. Most of us will seldom tell big lies about things like taxes or bills or affairs. Rather, we tell small lies about our abilities, our intentions, and who we truly are. If we do that long enough and become good enough at it, that is when we start losing our true selves and begin building our life on a foundation of deception, like Lana and Dave.

The Why of Lying

The first question we usually ask our children when they lie is, "Why? Why did you do that?" But we don't usually ask ourselves that question. Our children will lie to us for lots of reasons, but usually it comes down to one basic reason: to cover up what they did. As adults, our reasons get slightly more nuanced. First, we lie to rationalize or accommodate our failings and second, to avoid self-compassion (or, slowing down and dealing with our feelings). All of the types of lies and the reasons we lie only do one thing for us in the long run though: they inhibit growth.

Like I told Lana, and like it was with Lucifer, outward deception is almost always preceded by an inward lie. Why is honesty with ourselves so difficult at times? Because we are the only one on this earth who has access to our inner selves. It is easy to create a world within ourselves that requires little to no accountability. Outwardly we meet the minimal requirements of honesty, while inwardly we are constantly manipulating ourselves to our own demise and moving further away from becoming one with ourselves—and ultimately one with God.

Creating the Ladder of Lies

In counseling when I work with people who have spent significant amounts of time lying to themselves, I refer to this process as *Creating the Ladder of Lies*. The lies we tell ourselves, like the rungs of a ladder, build on each other and create the option to climb over our own healthy boundaries and avoid honest self-reflection. It is through these lies we access those things that will destroy us. It is not uncommon for people to come to counseling wanting to tell their compelling stories of why they are the way they are and justify their lack of growth. For awareness and spiritual or emotional growth to occur we must be willing to address our own self-manipulation and deception.

I will often ask a client to keep a journal of lies that they use to manipulate themselves. To start out, we will pick some of the simple lies they have been telling to themselves over the years that are fueling their actions. For example, a person who was once a victim of abuse may see themselves as a victim in life. Over time a series of lies has been used to maintain this perspective, and it is only through self-awareness and being transparent with themselves that they are able to overcome these self-deceptions.

Other lies my clients tell themselves over and over are ones that sound like this: *I'm not good enough, I'm not worth it, This is the last time I'll do this, I'll never change, No one will ever love me, I can't be forgiven.* We don't often like to think of these as lies or of ourselves as liars. However, if you find that your inner voice is telling you any of the above, you are telling yourself lies. This doesn't make you a bad person, but it does mean that if you want to grow you have to stop.

The Deceit of Justification

Justification of sin is also a big part of people's lives. Think back to Adam and Eve and how they reacted after they ate the fruit of the Tree of Knowledge of Good and Evil. God's first response to their transgression was to hold them accountable. Adam and Eve's first response was one of justification. The scriptural record tells us, "And He said, Who told thee that thou wast naked? Hast thou eaten of the tree, whereof I commanded thee that thou shouldest not eat? And the man said, The woman whom thou gavest to be with me, she gave me of the tree, and I did eat. And the Lord God said unto the woman, What is this that thou hast done? And the woman said, The serpent beguiled me, and I did eat" (Genesis 3:11–13).

Remember, though, that Adam and Eve were also faced with another choice in this moment, a choice between guilt and shame. Guilt, the feeling that we have done something against our beliefs and need to reconcile our actions with our values through making amends, is productive and can be a tool of the Holy Ghost to help us realign our life. If leveraged properly, guilt is typically not long-lasting, and God's love can still be felt. Shame, on the other hand, is the feeling that because we have done something wrong we ourselves *are* wrong. Shame encourages hiding and deceit, both with ourselves and with others. Shame thrives on secrets and grows over time. Shame consumes precious energy that could be focused on loving others and growth. It isolates us from others and most especially from God. Shame is always a dead-end.

When the Lord asked Adam and Eve what they had done they could have lied to God, and they could have lied to themselves. Their answer, "The serpent beguiled me, and I did eat" was a choice to be honest with God and with themselves. Eve could have justified her choice by playing the victim to the serpent or saying that her choice was okay through rationalization. Because they were able to avoid the traps of shame and move through the repentance process a second chance could be made available to them. The Lord quickly reassured them that there was a way for them to repent. He was their Father, He told them, and because He loved them He had provided a Savior.

How to Stop Self-Deception and Start the Process of Self-Acceptance

In the same way that Adam and Eve did, we need to move beyond deceit. We need to avoid lying to God and to ourselves. However, this isn't always easy. It takes a lot of self-awareness and courage to change this kind of habit. Lying to ourselves and others might feel safer, but it actually keeps us from accepting ourselves for who we are, which will only lead to more pain and shame. So how do we stop deceiving ourselves and start accepting ourselves?

The process is actually fairly straightforward. It involves four steps.

1. Awareness (become aware of when and how often you engage in self-deception)
2. Tell someone about it (confide in someone who can help you catch your self-deception and refute it)
3. Develop a truth statement (create a simple statement you can say to yourself when you are self-deceiving so you can remember to choose self-acceptance instead)
4. Remember who you are (A child of a Heavenly Father who loves you infinitely and supplied a Savior for you)

You can see that this process is similar to the well-known repentance process that we learn in Primary. In that process we typically think we have to recognize we sin, confess it, forsake it, and then make restitution. In the self-deception to self-acceptance process we follow four comparable steps, but instead of our focus being on what we are doing wrong and changing our behaviors, this process focuses on being aware of our weaknesses before we start and reframing our thoughts so we are less disposed to sin.

Now, this can be a bit complicated, so let me break it down.

Step One: Awareness

The first step to any change is to be aware of the need for change. Just like you listened to the voice in your head to help you recognize your own self-deception, you also need to learn how to turn down the voice in your head when it is telling you things that are not true. The

Ladder of Lies journal is a great way to identify the lies we have been manipulating ourselves with and remove the desire to use those lies in the future.

Usually the lies we tell ourselves are fairly common and sound a lot like the distorted thinking we talked about in the last chapter. If you find yourself thinking, *Well, that might be the way it is for everyone else but not for me*, that's self-deception. If you tend to be thinking, *Everyone else has it easy but me*, it's self-deception. Things like, "I'm not worth it." "There's no use trying." "It's not my fault. I couldn't help it." All of it is self-deception.

Step Two: Tell Someone about It

Everyone should have at least one trusted person in their lives that they can go to for honest insight and support. Maybe it's a sibling or your visiting teacher. Maybe it's a running or basketball buddy. It could even be your spouse. Bishops can sometimes fill this role also. Therapists or counselors are also a great choice.

Whoever it is you find, you need to tell them about self-deception in your life. How you are doing this? What kinds of lies do you tell yourself? How do you rationalize your mistakes and weaknesses so you don't have to change? Or, how you are overly hard on yourself, beating yourself up over and over for mistakes and weaknesses? Tell your trusted person what you have become aware of, and—this is the most important part—listen to their insights and perspectives. After all, self-deception is just that: deception to yourself. By its very nature this is a problem you cannot solve on your own.

Now, if the person you choose to confide in brings more shame into your life, then you should find a different person to talk to. However, you should expect to feel discomfort and frustration during this process. There will be days that you can hardly bring yourself to look in the mirror because you are so uncomfortable with what you are learning about yourself. But hang in there. Do not quit after the first two steps of this process. After all, giving up here is just another way of deceiving yourself. It's tantamount to saying, "I can't change. This is too hard. I'm not worth it. I don't deserve a better life." None of which are true.

Step Three: Develop a Truth Statement

Just like using correct thinking to keep distorted thinking in check, it's the same with self-deceit. The best thing you can do is check your deceit with truth.

To do this, start with your Ladder of Lies, and figure out what the most common lie is that you tell yourself. Try to go back to the first lie that you tell so that you can really get to the root of your problem. Then, examine that lie. Ask yourself how it serves you. After all, you wouldn't engage in self-deception if you weren't getting something out of it. There is a payoff to every behavior that you engage in. To stop the deceit, you have to figure out how you are trying to use the deceit to benefit you.

One of the most common benefits that I see people get from self-deceit is comfort. If they tell themselves that their problems are someone else's fault (such as "My kids have discipline problems because their teachers aren't doing enough" or "I would love to be able to hold down a calling, but my husband won't come home early enough from work so I can't"), they get to feel better about themselves and their choices. However, this comfort comes at the price of your personal growth.

Once you've figured out how it benefits you, you are ready to put together your Truth Statement. Your Truth Statement needs to do two things: first, it needs to refute the deceit, and second, it needs to state the truth that moves you forward. You need both parts so that you will be able to create a new mind-set that will provide a benefit that is either equal to the benefit you were getting from your self-deceit or greater.

If we go back to the example of blaming others for your current situation, then your truth statement might look something like this: *Even though my husband comes home from work late and that makes it difficult to hold a calling, I know that holding a calling is good for me, so I will try.* Or, if that statement is too long for you, make it shorter: *Even though it is hard, I will accept a calling because I can do hard things.* Need it even shorter? Try *I can do hard things.*

If the type of self-deceit you find yourself engaging in most often is the low self-esteem kind, then your truth statement will be different. For example, if you find yourself saying something along the lines of, "I'm not good enough. I'll never get any better. It's not worth it," then you need a truth statement that refutes that. It might be something like this:

My mistakes and failings don't define who I am; I can make mistakes and keep getting better; I can turn excrement into fertilizer. Or you could try something like, *I can keep getting better.*

Whatever you pick for your truth statement, write it down, and put it somewhere where you can see it often. Say it out loud to yourself. Even if you don't believe it at first, your mind will eventually start to see how what you are saying can be true, and your self-deceit will stop.

Step Four: Remember Who You Are

Odds are that if you have been engaging in self-deception, then your mind will probably balk at your truth statements. It will reject them, think around them, undermine them. To combat this you have to remember one of the most important truths that is emphasized in this book: who you really are.

First and foremost, you are a child of a loving Heavenly Father. He built this earth for you. He came up with a plan for you personally to progress and grow so you could become not just your best version of yourself but also an eternal, omnipotent version of yourself. He loves you so much that no matter what you have done He is always willing to reach out to you, to help you.

You are also a beloved brother or sister of the Savior of the entire world. Jesus Christ died for you personally. He atoned for your sins, weaknesses, mistakes, confusions, hurts, angers, transgressions, and loneliness. He intimately knows your thoughts and your heart. And He loves you.

He, and your Heavenly Father, love you regardless of your past and regardless of your future. Their love for you is whole; they only ask for your honesty and humility. Their love for you is eternal. It will never end. They love you so much that what they want more than anything is to be with you in every moment to guide you, comfort you, and hold you. They want to be with you *now,* regardless of what your now looks like. Christ promised us, "I will not leave you comfortless: I will come to you" (John 14:18).

Remember, Their love will support your statements of truth and allow you to see yourself through a new lens. There is no clearer way to truth than through the all-powerful love of God.

The End of Deception Is the Beginning of Peace

Conflict ends when we stop seeking to justify ourselves by lying to ourselves. When we stop deceiving ourselves and relying on justifications and untruths to rationalize our actions or non-actions we open ourselves to peace. This peace comes primarily through allowing Christ to be more a part of our everyday moments. His Atonement and love becomes proactive in our lives. We are not proving anything to Him or hiding anything from Him. We are simply receiving Him in to our life now. Can you imagine any more peaceful way to live?

In Doctrine and Covenants 38:27, Jesus said, "I say unto you, be one; and if ye are not one ye are not mine." For the longest time I interpreted this verse as a statement of group unification but I now see it as something more. Christ recognizes our potential to be in conflict with ourselves. He sees the battle inside every person: our physical being battling with our spiritual being, our intellectual being struggling with our emotional being. He knows that we are often distracted from the important things of heaven and earth because of these internal conflicts. He is aware that unless we are able to become one with ourselves, we will have little chance of becoming one with each other or with God, and it is our own self-deception and self-justification that fuels these internal conflicts.

If accountability and repentance do not happen after a sin or mistake is committed, it is not uncommon to see people rewriting their beliefs and values to accommodate their actions. As a bishop I witnessed this on a number of occasions. Few of us are comfortable with the discomfort that comes from being out-of-alignment with ourselves. Many people are willing to rewrite their values instead of humbly embracing Christ to aid them in their struggle, mostly because they don't know how. We open the door to Christ and our Father's Holy Spirit when we stop self-deception.

In his talk "Lord, Is It I?" President Dieter F. Uchtdorf says:

> None of us likes to admit when we are drifting off the right course. Often we try to avoid looking deeply into our souls and confronting our weaknesses, limitations, and fears. Consequently, when we do examine our lives, we look through the filter of biases, excuses, and

> stories we tell ourselves in order to justify unworthy thoughts and actions. But being able to see ourselves clearly is essential to our spiritual growth and well-being. If our weaknesses and shortcomings remain obscured in the shadows, then the redeeming power of the Savior cannot heal them and make them strengths. Ironically, our blindness toward our human weaknesses will also make us blind to the divine potential that our Father yearns to nurture within each of us.[1]

The only true justification comes through Jesus Christ. No matter how strategic or powerful our self-justifications seem to us, they will never be effective. We simply cannot justify ourselves.

In order for us to access the light and love of God we must first learn to be accountable to ourselves. When we experience feelings of guilt, we must be willing to follow the path of accountability and light (God's path) not the path of shame and secrets (Lucifer's path). We will never be free until we choose to be aware of our self-deceptions and act in accordance with that light. "And ye shall know the truth and the truth shall set you free" (John 8:32). That is the promise of Christ's Atonement *now.*

Note

1. Dieter F. Uchtdorf, "Lord, Is It I?" *Ensign*, November 2014, 56–59.

Part Three

Take Up Your Bed

When Jesus saw him lie, and knew that he had been now a long time in that case, he saith unto him, Wilt thou be made whole?

The impotent man answered him, Sir, I have no man, to put me into the pool; but while I am coming, another steppeth down before me.

Jesus saith unto him, Rise, ***take up thy bed.***

—John 5:6–8

Desires dictate our priorities, priorities shape our choices, and choices determine our actions. The desires we act on determine our changing, our achieving, and our becoming.

—Dallin H. Oaks

("Desire," *Ensign*, May 2011, 42.)

Chapter 9
Be Still and Breathe

Carolyn came back after about a month with a declaration. "Outside-in doesn't work. I knew that before, but I guess I just had to make sure. Let's try inside out. I've got a list of the cognitive distortions I think I use the most. Is this where the real work starts?"

I couldn't help but smile. This was two of Carolyn's worlds colliding. Her planning and over-achieving self had decided to take action, but her honest and exhausted self was guiding what type of action to take.

We looked over the list and talked about what she could do to combat the cognitive distortions. She took notes and thoughtfully nodded a lot. Near the end of our hour I paused and asked her a question. "How do you feel about all this? This is a pretty big list."

"I can handle this. I'll just do whatever it takes to get this done. We give this a couple weeks, and I'll have it down." Her jaw was set, and her eyes were scanning the list over and over.

"Let's pause for a minute, Carolyn. Line upon line, right? Trying to tackle this in a matter of weeks misses the point."

"Again? I'm not lying to myself again, am I?"

"No. You're not lying to yourself, but the point of this isn't to do this fast and fix you up so you can get back to the rat race. Therapy isn't some sort of pit stop on the treadmill of success. The point is to give you a set of tools to help you navigate difficult moments as they come. Because no matter how quickly and effectively you master your cognitive distortions you won't ever be fixed. There is no fixing you because you aren't broken. You're not a problem to be solved. You're a person."

"Right. I'm a person. A child of God. I got it. What does that have to do with this?" She gestured to the list of distortions.

"Carolyn, how often do you just stop?"

"Huh? Never. I mean, I sleep each night, but I can't stop. There isn't time. This life is the time to prepare to meet God, right? We're supposed to be anxiously engaged, right? If we want to live our lives the way God expects us to, we can't stop and rest on our laurels. We've got to keep working."

"Okay. I guess that's one way to look at, it but I don't think that's necessarily true. Do you think God spends His eternity racing from one task to the next? Do you get the impression that Jesus, even though He knew His time was limited, was ever in a hurry?"

"No . . ."

"And isn't the real point of this life, all the good things we do, to help us and others to become more like our Heavenly Father and our Savior?"

"Yes . . ."

"So, how does pushing yourself so hard to go so fast accomplish that?"

Carolyn was stumped. "I really don't know."

"That's because it doesn't. Orientation is everything, speed is relative. You've got to take time to sit still and breathe. Even Jesus Christ found time to do that. Do you think you can follow His example that way and learn to be still?"

She gave a little harumph *of defeat. "I guess I'd better try."*

Lana was agitated. We'd chosen a mantra for her to help her change her thoughts and stay connected to sources of her true worth but she was still occasionally struggling with past memories. Staying away from Jared in those times was especially hard. Not cutting was even harder. She tried to focus on her kids and her job and plan for the future but she still couldn't picture a future. On days like today, when her past was so overwhelming, she could barely comprehend tomorrow, let alone two months or two years from now.

"Where are you today, Lana?"

"Huh?" She broke her staring contest with the window to glance at me.

"You're lost to me today. There's something distracting you. What's up?"

"I don't know. It doesn't make any sense. I don't know how to explain it. It's just like there's this memory of people I can't quite place, and they keep saying stuff, and it feels like it's happening right now except that I know I'm in your office but I don't feel like I am."

I nodded not quite sure where this was going. "Do you want to talk about the memory, or do you think it will go away?"

"I don't know. It's not even a real memory. Just a feeling. Just this part of me that knows something bad is going to happen soon, and I just keep getting scared, and sometimes I can hear them talking, but I don't know who they are. I'm just not safe anywhere right now, James."

"Okay. So let's try putting it on the shelf."

"James, it's just a feeling. I can't set it on the shelf."

"I don't mean a literal shelf. I mean a mental shelf. Just assign that feeling an object and then we'll put that object on a mental shelf labeled 'to deal with later.'"

She stared at me blankly. "I'm allowed to do that?"

"Yeah. You are."

"I thought therapy was all about, like, facing your deepest darkest stuff and overcoming it and whatever."

"It is. Except when it isn't. My goal for you, Lana, and I hope this is your goal too, is that you can wake up each morning and not worry so much about your past, not be haunted by it. I want you to wake up and not worry about your future and what is going to happen next. I want you to wake up and think, 'Today is a day when I can do great things to create the life I want. I'm going to work right now, each moment, to become who God wants me to be.' That's what therapy is all about. Is fixating on this feeling-memory going to do that?"

"No."

"Then let's put it on the shelf and just take a minute to breathe."

"I'm bad at breathing. How many times do I need to tell you that?"

"Let's try to put the feeling on the shelf and work on the breathing."

Lana nodded, took a breath of her own accord, and said, "Okay."

The Power of Stillness

A favorite hymn begins, "Be still, my soul: the Lord is on thy side; With patience bear thy cross of grief or pain." In its second verse it continues, "Thy God doth undertake to guide the future as he has the past."[1] The Psalmist reminds us that Heavenly Father hopes we will "be still, and know that I am God" (Psalm 46:10). When the Apostles were out on the sea late at night, a terrible tempest beset them, Christ's command to the waters was simple and powerful, "Be still" (Mark 4:39).

Do you see the theme? There's something about stillness that opens us up to God's power in a way that nothing else can. However, our modern world doesn't naturally allow for a lot of stillness so it seems unnatural or lazy to us.

Our modern age has created a new phenomenon that some experts are calling *popcorn brain.*[2] Popcorn brain is the effect of having so many options, usually technology-based, open to us all the time. Some researchers believe that this constant interaction with technologies can actually change the way the brain is wired, making it harder to sustain attention, identify emotion, and perform cognitive functions.[3] This shows up most in our ability to interact with others in meaningful ways and to accomplish our goals. We end up busier and busier but getting fewer and fewer things done, leaving us more and more stressed, which can propel us to become even busier than we were to begin with. It's a vicious circle that creates emotional unrest.

To combat this we have to make a conscious choice to stop multitasking and start rebuilding our abilities to be still, to do just one thing at a time, to engage in less stimulation, and to really focus on what is happening *now.*

To put it another way, think about the workplace and your first reaction: when we encounter difficulties and stress there, we often feel the need to work harder, not necessarily smarter. If you are trying to bail out a boat, it won't matter how fast you bail if you never plug the hole.

It's the same with our lives. It isn't always better to do more things faster. In fact, it's almost *never* better to do more things faster. We need to slow down, breathe, and focus on what will help us in the big picture, not just the immediate moment.

The Mental Effects of Stillness

Remember when we talked about the primal and the higher brain? The primal brain is the one that is the source of our instincts and knee-jerk reactions. The higher brain is the one that overrides those instincts and reactions by helping us make wise decisions. I bet you can guess which one is in charge when we are multitasking.

More often than not, multitasking feels like it should be run by our higher brains. After all, that's where the organizational thinking and planning happens. But when we have to juggle so many things at once it triggers the stress response in our bodies, which causes the primal brain to come to attention. Then, before we realize it, it's not our higher brain running the show any more. We're running scared and stressed through our to-do lists just like a gazelle runs across the savannah when a lion is close behind.

Contrast that with a state I like to call *flow*. When you are in flow, you are completely absorbed in the task at hand. Everything else around you drops away and fades to the background, like in a movie. Time seems to slow and, if you're lucky, disappear. Artists find flow when they paint. Writers find it when they write. Musicians when they play. Runners when they run. Some people find it when they are doing woodwork or baking or dancing. Others might find it when they are reading or even cleaning. Like a moving meditation, flow clears your mind and your heart. In that state concentration isn't an effort, and your best work appears. Flow is the ultimate higher state.

To get to flow, though, we have to slow down.

Some interesting things happen in our bodies when we slow down and breathe. That stillness actually has an immediate effect on the body. We know that stress triggers different processes in your body. Stillness is similar, but it does the opposite.

The minute you pause and breathe your body starts to relax. Oxygen floods your brain increasing cognitive energy, your heartbeat slows, and your blood pressure decreases and slows down the production of stress hormones. Some studies even show that conscious, deep breathing can help with chronic illness.[4]

All of this breathing helps us better regulate our thoughts and our moods. It keeps our higher brain at the helm and makes sure our lower brain doesn't take over. We can settle into a state of optimum effort, where the effort we are expending is just the right amount for what we need to get done. We can better sort out our priorities. We can, in actuality, just go with the flow.

The Spiritual Effects of Stillness

The powerful reviving and rejuvenating effects of stillness on our physical and mental health are just the beginning. In actuality, greater health in these areas sets the stage for greater health in an even more important area of our lives. Stillness is what ushers in deep, lasting spiritual power.

In a 2014 devotional, M. Russell Ballard posed an important question in relation to our modern age of technology. He said, "Seemingly, as our world gets brighter, louder, and busier, we have a greater challenge feeling the Spirit in our lives. If your life is void of quiet time, would you begin tonight to seek for some?"[5]

The difference between a hard worker and a smart worker is that the smart worker knows that being still may be the right answer at times, whereas the hard worker feels compelled to use action to deal with all situations. After all, it's like my wife counsels me when I have to clean the stove: you can scrub that baked-on grease as hard as you want until it goes away, or you can spray the cleaner on it, wait for a bit, and come back and scrub it when it is softened and ready to be wiped off.

Quiet time works for our spiritual selves the way cleaner works on the stove. When we commit to turning off distractions and noise and simply sit and breathe, we give our brains the opportunity to check in with our hearts and our spirit. It is then that we will find the inspiration and prompting we need to really take care of our problems. Remember in the Old Testament when Elijah was commanded to seek the Lord on a mountaintop, and a great wind came by? The Lord was not in the wind. Nor was the Lord in the earthquake and fire that followed. Instead He was in a still, small voice that came after all the upheaval. Spiritual solutions to problems rarely require as much elbow grease as we think. What is really required is that we simply slow down. If we are constantly in a whirlwind of busyness, how will we hear our Father in Heaven?

Operating on the Godly Frequency

When I was a kid growing up in California, I spent a lot of time trying to find music on the radio. It was the 1970s, and if I wanted to hear that awesome The Doors song or the Bee Gees grooving it out, I had to sit at the radio and painstakingly turn the dial. The stations broadcasted from specific frequencies, but it was only through carefully moving the dial that you could hone in on the signal. To my young mind it seemed like anything could disrupt the signal from a bird flying by to my mom cooking in the kitchen. I had to be perfectly still and just focus on the minute movements of the dial and what sounds I could decipher through the static.

To hear our Father in Heaven's voice, to feel our Savior's love and guidance, we have to tune ourselves to what I've come to think of as *the Godly Frequency*. After all, we know that the Lord is always broadcasting His love to us but that signal can, sometimes, be easily disrupted. If we want to operate on that Godly Frequency, we have to be still so we can focus on the minute adjustments we need to make in our hearts so we can be in tune.

In a critical dialogue with His Apostles following His death and resurrection, Jesus said, "And, behold, I send the promise of my Father upon you: but tarry ye in the city of Jerusalem, until ye be endued with power from on high" (Luke 24:49). The Apostles—like Elijah, like us—had to hold still. They needed to tarry in one place until they were given the spiritual gifts they needed to accomplish the massive work God had for them. After all, they were soon to be commanded to take the good news of Christ's gospel to the entire world in an age where transportation and communication options were sorely limited, and they, as individuals, were hated.

Likewise, our ability to be still, breathe, and receive God's spirit and directions for us will be critical in our ability to meet the demands of life. If we are running on empty while trying to work, take care of our families, serve in our callings, and take care of the million small things that make up our day-to-day lives, we will end up taking a nosedive. Not because too much was asked of us, but because we have not learned how to be still and oscillate on the Godly Frequency.

For so many of us, much of our energy is spent dealing with the logistics and conflicts of the day. The assumption is, when we solve this next problem, then we will slow down and get some replenishment. What we fail to recognize is that unless we have a method for regular replenishment—not tomorrow, but now—we will not be able to deal with the conflicts and logistics of the day. Being replenished often means just being still and breathing and receiving what God is offering us. This is the ultimate state of flow, where you and God are working together in a cycle of peace and abundance.

Experimenting with Stillness

Because stillness is so foreign to our modern lives, you might be unnerved at the idea. For many of my clients, asking them to be still is tantamount to asking them to walk across hot coals or lay on a bed of nails. Sure, they've heard that it can be a transcendent experience, and they know other people can do it, but it doesn't seem like something they can do.

The best way to figure out stillness, I tell them, is to simply experiment. Most people want a method or a checklist to be still. They want to *do* something to make them still. You see the irony there, right? Stillness is the opposite of doing. To be still you just have to, well, be still. However, stillness looks different for every person, so you'll have to play around a bit.

Sometimes the best way to figure out what something is, is to figure out what it is not. So try this. Place your hand over your mouth and nose and hold your breath for as long as you can and see what happens. Do your best to notice what is happening in your body right now, in this moment.

At first, when the breath is limited, most people try to distract themselves from not breathing. But eventually taking that next breath will become the most important thing in your life. The longer you go without breathing the more important breathing will become and the more anxious you will become to get it right now.

Nothing connects us to the now more than breathing. There is also nothing better than breathing to help us create stillness in ourselves. By combining stillness and breathing, we orient ourselves in the now, and we are able to be replenished through God's spirit.

Let's experiment now. Sit down with your legs uncrossed and your feet resting comfortably on the floor. Roll your shoulders back, tilt your chin slightly up, and lift your sternum. Now take a conscious breath through your nose and imagine the air moving down to completely fill your lungs from the bottom up. Notice your belly expanding and your chest rising until your lungs are comfortably full. Hold that fullness for a short moment, and now gently let the breath out your mouth. Do that a few more times.

How do you feel? Most likely, the scattered tightness that came from not breathing is completely gone. Your mind probably feels clearer. Your energy level is probably a bit higher. You may even feel some muscle tension draining from your shoulders and neck and chest. That is the effect of stillness. That is the sensation you are looking for.

Other experiments to try to create stillness include:

- Taking a walk—without your phone or any other devices
- Looking out the window and observing nature
- Lying underneath a tree watching the leaves move in the breeze
- Sitting on the couch with the TV and all other distractions off
- Lying in bed and reciting a single line of scripture over and over in your head
- Kneeling down as you are going to pray but simply saying, "Father in Heaven, I'm here." Then wait.
- Pausing for three seconds before responding to a question or request
- Practicing yoga or other gentle stretching
- Engaging in meditation guides or apps (there's a million of them out there—odds are you can find one that will work for you)

Nothing on that list is remarkable or new. In fact, you probably remember doing most of them when you were a kid (remember how much less stress you had then?). The key to these is to experiment with them until you know what works for you. What takes your stress level down? Which one helps clear the way for you to connect to the Godly Frequency? Remember, this isn't something to add to your to-do list. It should be as simple as breathing.

Stillness for the Long Haul

Now, it wasn't a coincidence that the Savior chose to teach His disciples about stillness when the tempest was raging around them. It wasn't a coincidence that Elijah heard the voice of the Lord shortly after a whirlwind, earthquake, and fire. Our lives consist of upheavals. There's no way around the fact that work, hardship, stress, and adversity exist in our lives. After all, that's part of the plan. We know we were sent to earth to be tested and tried.

There will be many moments in our lives that we feel like we are in the bottom of the ninth with two outs. Our first instinct in those moments will be to avoid and distract and get busier and busier trying to fix things. But in truth these are the moments we need to be most present in. Those are the moments we need to slow down and breathe. We need to be still to allow ourselves the opportunity to find the Godly Frequency. It is only then, as we begin to resonate on that frequency regardless of the possible disruptions, that we commune with God and discover peace in the midst of the storm.

That is the power of stillness: to take our roughest seas, our scariest tempests and whirlwinds, and make them ripples on the surfaces of our lives.

It all starts with a simple choice, to just be, right here, right now.

Notes

1. "Be Still My Soul," *Hymns*, no. 124.
2. Elizabeth Cohen, "Does Life Online Give You 'Popcorn Brain'?" CNN, June 23, 2011, accessed September 03, 2018, http://www.cnn.com/2011/HEALTH/06/23/tech.popcorn.brain.ep/index.html?eref=rss_health&utm_source=feedburner&utm_medium=feed&utm_campaign=Feed: rss/cnn_health (RSS: Health).
3. Ibid.
4. Gretchen Cuda, "Just Breathe: Body Has a Built-in Stress Reliever." NPR, December 06, 2010, accessed September 03, 2018, http://www.npr.org/2010/12/06/131734718/just-breathe-body-has-a-built-in-stress-reliever.
5. M. Russell Ballard, "Be Still, and Know That I Am God," CES Devotional for Young Adults, May 4, 2014.

Chapter 10
Be Fearless and Embrace Opportunity

Dave was rapidly improving in some ways but in others his life wasn't going where he wanted it to. He and Julie were still separated. She let him know that she had a lawyer and that she was close to filing for a divorce. He only saw the kids once a week, and some of them seemed mad at him no matter what he did. He was afraid of what Julie did or didn't say to them about him. He had no way of knowing what they knew about his struggles, and he certainly wasn't going to bring it up.

Most days he was more hopeful than he ever had been, but it still seemed like there were far too many days he was white-knuckling his way through the pornography temptations. They came to his memory when he was stressed or tired, or sometimes he would dream them, waking up in a frenzy, unsure of what to do. Most of the time he fell back on the strategies we mapped out for changing the station in his mind, but he wasn't always successful.

It seemed like Dave needed more support in his life. "How are things going with the addiction recovery group? You haven't mentioned that in a while."

Dave sighed, "Yeah. I only go intermittently. I don't say much. I still haven't gotten through all the steps."

"Really? Which one are you on?"

Looking slightly sheepish, he replied, "The Fearless Moral Inventory. Still. In my mind I've taken to calling it the FearFUL Moral Inventory."

"Ah. I see. Well, maybe we should work on it together again. There's no reason I can't help you get it started."

Dave looked like he was going to be sick. "Are you sure? I mean, can't we just go back to, I don't know, practicing something we've worked on before? Or maybe we can just talk about fishing," he joked thinly.

"Let's give it a try." I pulled out my copy of the Addiction Recovery Program and read to him. After listening to the options for how to do it, Dave decided to put his together chronologically. We also decided to focus mostly on the memories that brought him shame, similar to the way using pornography made him feel.

I handed him a paper and pen so he could start writing as we talked. Dave's hands were literally shaking as he picked up the pen.

"Dave, what are you afraid is going to happen as a result of this inventory?"

"I don't know. It seems like such a dumb thing to be afraid of. When I can't sleep at night, this is basically what my brain is doing anyway. Making a list of all the stupid things I've done, all the reasons I'm in the situation I'm in."

"Wait, Dave, check your thoughts. Are you being present without judgment?"

"No. I'm not."

"Is it that judgment that is creating your fear?"

"Maybe. But I just, I don't know. I don't know how to push through it. My brain shuts down. I can't think. I just want to hide."

"And look at porn?"

"Maybe. Yes, sometimes."

"It sounds like we need to do some work on managing fear then. Let's get started."

There were occasions when Lana came into my office happy, no storms at all in her eyes or mind. Today was one of those days, a good day. She started talking first.

"I've slept better the whole last week. I do that deep breathing thing you taught me at night when the bad feelings start. It totally helps."

"Bad feelings? Check your judgment, Lana."

"Right. Scary feelings. Is that better?" she said, giving me a thumbs up.

"Yes." I smiled, "Is the sleep why you are feeling so good today?"

"Yeah. Partly. But I think a lot of it has to do with another decision I've made."

I listened as she told me of one particularly frustrating night, when her fears were getting the best of her, and she finally got fed up.

"James, it was crazy. And not like in my normal crazy way. I know, I know. I'm not supposed to call myself crazy, but just listen. Like, I was lying in bed shaking and wishing all the memories, all the bad stuff, would all just go away, and I was just hating everything, myself included. And then, clear as a bell, there was a voice in my head that was like, 'ENOUGH. I have had enough.' I don't know if it was me or the Spirit or both or what, but it felt like I turned a corner in my head. So I said it out loud. It felt so good to draw that line, to say, 'Enough.' And then I made a decision. I'm not living in fear anymore. Fear doesn't get to make my decisions. I do. So next time I'm afraid of something, I'm going to do it. No matter what."

This was typical Lana in action. She was an energetic person, when she had enough sleep, and she was usually an all-in kind of girl. She did things big, and if she was done with fear then she was going to be done. It was exciting—and a little nerve wracking. I could see this going in a good direction or leading to a bad one.

"What do you mean by that exactly?" I started. "Sometimes fear is your brain actually trying to protect you. I mean, we call the lower brain the lizard brain *because it's been evolutionarily evolved to protect you from harm. Just like a lizard knows to run away when a predator is coming, your brain does that too."*

"Right. I know that. But my brain does it too much, James. Way too much. I mean, didn't you tell me one time that I'm as safe as I decide to be? It's my thoughts and judgments that are creating the level of fear I live with. I'm done hiding all the time. For the next year, at least, I'm going to say yes *to the opportunities that come my way, even if I'm scared. Especially if I'm scared. Unless it goes against what I believe in. Like, I'm not going to start drinking or something just because I haven't ever done it."*

She knitted her brow in thought. As a victim of abuse, boundaries were hard for Lana. So often in her life she wasn't allowed to have her own boundaries, and when she did the abusers in her life destroyed them. Creating and maintaining healthy boundaries that would be beneficial to her was a new concept. This idea of developing boundaries to facilitate growth not just avoid pain appeared to be overwhelming to Lana.

Afraid her resolve was going to give way, I jumped in. "True. You don't avoid alcohol because you're afraid of it. Why do you avoid it?"

She thought for another minute. "Well, like, I don't drink alcohol because I believe that avoiding it is good for me. Like the Word of Wisdom says."

"What do we call that when you know how you feel and think about something and act accordingly?"

She opened her eyes wide at the question. She wasn't sure. We hadn't talked about this in a long time.

"A boundary? Is that right? It's easy to make a decision about alcohol because my belief in the Word of Wisdom is a boundary I've set in my life. If that's what a boundary is, then maybe those are easier than I realized."

A New Message from Fear

I used to stay up watching Johnny Carson. For years, it was part of my evening ritual to wind down the day. One night a guest said something like this to Johnny, "I wasn't really alive until I had my first original thought." Johnny seemed a bit confused by this statement, but I knew exactly what the man meant, which is why the statement has stuck with me all these years.

A few months earlier I had had my first original thought. I was about twenty-four years old at the time, and my thought was this: *When I feel the feelings of fear or discomfort in a new situation maybe that is God trying to tell me there is an opportunity straight ahead.* This set off a cascade of other new thoughts: *What if I step forward instead of stepping back when I feel these feelings? What if I decide to see those uncomfortable feelings as feelings of encouragement and act on them—how would my life change?*

When this new thought crystallized in my mind I decided to experiment on it. Over the next few months I found that my life was rich with opportunities. As others were stepping back, I was stepping forward. Instead of letting fear limit me, I was turning it into a catalyst. In a few short months of intense experimentation, I realized my life would never be the same. I felt so alive. I felt more present than I had ever felt. This was what living in the now felt like.

It was awesome.

The Veil of Fear

As time passed this simple thought became a belief system. I started to see that almost all growth moments in life were camouflaged in fear. I started to refer to this as *the veil of fear*. Paul said to Timothy, "For God hath not given us the spirit of fear; but of power, and of love, and of a sound mind" (2 Timothy 1:7). Fear works a little bit like the veil we went through when we came to earth. Just as our previous experiences and memories were covered by the veil when we were born, fear often covers up opportunity and makes it appear scary. With the veil at birth the purpose was to help us learn and grow. The veil of fear, on the other hand, is an imposter of that veil. It seeks not to help us but rather to hold us back. That's how we know it is, sometimes, a tool of Lucifer.

I don't often talk about Old Scratch, since I believe our choices are always more powerful than he is, but fear is one of Satan's most powerful tactics, and he uses it to his advantage often. Think about all the times you want to do something positive (apologize after a fight, give someone a pass-along card, try a new activity) and you don't because of fear. He whispers to us, "It's too hard, too painful, too uncomfortable. People will laugh at you, you will be mocked, and you will feel embarrassed." Much the same way those in the great and spacious building mocked the followers of Christ. "And I also cast my eyes round about, and beheld, on the other side of the river of water, a great and spacious building; and it stood as it were in the air, high above the earth. And it was filled with people, both old and young, both male and female; and their manner of dress was exceedingly fine; and they were in the attitude of mocking and pointing their fingers towards those who had come at and were partaking of the fruit" (1 Nephi 8:26–27).

Lucifer is a little bit trickier, though. He not only gets other people to sometimes laugh or mock, he gets us to use phrases against ourselves like "I'm too shy" or "I'm comfortable where I'm at" or "I don't like new things." If he can get us to say these things to ourselves, he can get us to back away from the veil of fear instead of pushing through it. That's part of why it is so important that we conquer the voices in our heads and make them our ally like we talked about earlier.

The Opposite of Fear

Lucifer knows that as we conquer more by stepping through the veil of fear, our faith will grow stronger, opportunities will increase for us, and his influence in our lives will dramatically decrease. Our Heavenly Father also understands the importance of us overcoming fear in our life. This is why the first principle of the gospel is faith in Jesus Christ. Faith in Him proclaims that we believe Christ has overcome all and that He is with us as we pass through every trial and hardship in our lives, every veil of fear. In the Garden of Gethsemane Jesus said to His Father, "if thou be willing, remove this cup from me: nevertheless not my will, but thine, be done" (Luke 22:42). Jesus too had to pass through veils of fear, and He did so by exercising faith in His Father. We too must pass through veils of fear by exercising faith in Christ and our Father in Heaven right now.

Just as we gained power as we passed through the veil of birth and received our mortal bodies, and we will receive more knowledge and power when we pass back through the veil to Heavenly Father's presence, when we pass through veils of fear we are empowered to do more. It is the only way to progress. Think how much your growth would have been stunted if you had chosen to stay behind in the premortal life instead of embracing the possibly frightening next step in your eternal journey? When you let fear run your life now, you are losing the same type of growth opportunities.

As we live a life of fear, we increase our worry of the future just waiting for the next shoe to drop. Additionally, fear will start us believing that our weaknesses define who we are. Soon, our life begins to fill with disappointment. In time, fear robs us of the now, and we are filled with anxiety and regret. However, through faith in Christ, the opposite happens. We are able to demonstrate not only our willingness to conquer veils of fear in our lives but also to actually live with less fear. With each veil of fear we step through, using the power of Christ and His Atonement, we claim our now and become present again in our own lives.

What is amazing about this process is that as we choose faith it eventually turns into something much more powerful: love. Christ tells us that there is no fear in love because, "Perfect love casteth out fear" (1 John 4:18). As we choose to act in faith, our lives fill with God's perfect, eternal love, and we are empowered to cast our fears behind us. Our worries about the past and our anxieties about the future fade. This then empowers us to act with more faith, thereby bringing more of God's love into our lives. This is the kind of cycle we want to be in! One that exponentially increases our faith, love, and joy in the now.

Distinguishing Fear That Saves Us from Fear That Cages Us

Now, before we jump too quickly out of our comfort zones or throw caution entirely to the wind, we need to learn to discern something important. We need to stop and figure out how to recognize the legitimate fears that come from either our minds or the Holy Ghost and will keep us safe and those fears that simply hold us back. These can sometimes be easily confused in our minds, especially if we are used to being anxious. Thankfully, by asking ourselves a few simple questions we can easily distinguish healthy fear from unhealthy fear.

Does this fear impede my growth as an individual? This is the most straightforward litmus test for fear. If you avoid something you are afraid of, will it keep you from becoming a better version of yourself? If the answer is yes, then it is an unhealthy fear, and it is one you need to overcome. For example, if your fear is one of public speaking then you might refuse to give a talk at church. However, by refusing to give that talk you are losing an opportunity to learn more about a gospel topic and have the Holy Ghost specifically guide you. You are also robbing others of the opportunity to hear your thoughts and learn things that only you can teach. That definitely impedes your growth. You've got to get over that one.

Does this fear increase my opportunities in the future or limit them? This one is a little bit trickier. Let's use a fear of heights for this example. Maybe whenever you get to a high point on a mountain or can see a view from a top floor of a tall building, you start to get sick inside and worry about falling and dying. Well, this fear could be a healthy one. It will probably keep you from walking too close to the edge of a cliff or being dangerous when on a rooftop. By listening to that fear you are keeping a lot of opportunities open for your future by not dying or hurting yourself. That's a healthy fear. However, if that fear keeps you from taking an elevator to a higher floor so you can do your job better than it is limiting your opportunities. Overcoming this kind of fear is good. The best way to know if a fear is getting the best of you and keeping you from growing is to ask yourself this question, "Is the fear serving me or am I serving the fear?"

Does this fear seem rational to other people around me? Now, this question isn't the best one to start with because the opinions that matter most are that of yourself and Heavenly Father. But when it comes to fear sometimes we need to use the population at large as a reality check on our own worries. A good example of this one is a fear of flying. You might be the kind of person who is petrified by the idea of having to climb into a metal tube and go hurtling across the sky at a gajillion miles an hour because, duh, doesn't that sound crazy? But, like many others, you are probably also the kind of person who needs to fly on occasion. So, you have to ask yourself, even though your brain is telling you that flying could harm you, looking at all the people around you will help you see how irrational that fear really is. After all, while many people are afraid of flying very few people actually get hurt or die due to planes. That kind of fear is an unhealthy one because it isn't based in reality.

What does Heavenly Father want for me? This is probably the single most powerful question out of the bunch. Fear is something that grows from a hyper-focus on minutiae. By backing ourselves out of that perspective and trying to take a more eternal, heavenly view we can save ourselves a lot of pain and worry. Remember, it doesn't matter what your fear is, God doesn't ever want you shaking, afraid, and immobilized. He wants you to feel strong, empowered, and capable. He wants you to feel like you are the daughter or son of the King of Heaven and that you are meant to do great things. If your fear makes you feel small or stuck, it is an unhealthy one. If it is one that helps you draw boundaries and make choices that bring you closer to the vision Heavenly Father has for you, then it is a healthy one. And, really, at that point, if you are truly seeing things from Heavenly Father's perspective, it won't be scary to you anymore. It will simply be undesirable.

In many ways fear simply comes down to a cost-benefit analysis, where the cost of moving through our fears is so much higher than the pain of staying afraid and choosing to do nothing. However, when we ask ourselves the above questions we can view our fears from a broader lens and start to see the true costs and benefits. Almost every time, pushing through our fears will bring a big payout in the long run.

Most Common Veils of Fear

Those examples above are pretty specific and are great for illustrating how to evaluate healthy fears and unhealthy fears, but most fear is not that specific. Part of how fear works is that it is unspecific, mysterious, hard to pin down. It's just a gut feeling that clutches at us. So, as we figure out how to overcome fear I am going to talk about categories of fear. This will make it easier for you to figure out how to adapt the techniques to your own lives.

There are a few common categories of veils of fear that most of us encounter on a regular basis. We do not often recognize that these moments are a test of our faith. However, as mundane as they may seem, they are definitely significant to our growth and embracing the now. Let's look at each of them individually.

Veil Number One: Fear of Failure versus the Love of Experience

This is probably the single most common fear on earth. If you take just a minute you can probably think of nearly a dozen times you didn't do something because you were afraid you might fail at it. All of us have unwritten novels, unsung songs, dates we didn't go on, teams we didn't try out for, callings we didn't accept, jobs we didn't apply for, or experiences we missed simply because we were afraid we would fail.

The fear of doing something badly is so common entire books are written about how to work around it or push through it or overcome it. A quick amazon.com search reveals over two hundred titles about dealing with fear. I'm sure many of these books have excellent advice and are extremely helpful. I am also sure that all of them have one principle in common: something has to be more valuable to you than your fear, and that something is the experience that comes from taking action. You have to want and love the experience that you will gain more than you fear the failure, or the consequences of failure, that could possibly happen.

One place we see this manifest fairly clearly in the Church and in my therapy office is in relationships. So many people are afraid of failing at long-term relationships and marriage that they avoid them altogether. Now, sometimes there are legitimate reasons to be afraid. The effects of abuse, bad examples from our families of origin, and destructive relationships are real and powerful. It makes sense in some ways to be afraid of getting hurt again. However, God's plan for families and happiness in this life and the next hasn't changed. It is still based on relationships between individuals and those individuals choosing to form families. Is there a real risk of failure? Absolutely! Many marriages end in divorce, and even those that don't experience heartache and stress. Hanging in there with no guarantees and working on your marriage will, at times, take a lot of effort and focus. For many that seems like an extremely high risk.

However, the payout of risking on a relationship and marriage and family comes in the form of priceless experiences that will help you grow in ways that nothing else can. Will you make mistakes as a boyfriend or girlfriend? You bet. Will you struggle as a spouse? Of course. Will you feel overwhelmed and incompetent as a parent? Absolutely! However, engaging in these roles is also one of the only ways to feel, learn, and give unconditional love. The experience of sticking with a significant other through hard times is like no other experience. Going to bed with and waking up next to the same person every day for years and years is unique. The ups and downs of parenting will create in you a fortitude and wisdom that is like no other. The value of those experiences far outweighs the price of failure.

Focus on the value of the experiences you will gain, not the possibility of failure.

Veil Number Two: Fear of Repentance versus a Love of God

Closely related to the fear of failure is the fear of repentance. After all, if we weren't afraid of fixing our mistakes we probably wouldn't be so afraid of making them. However, most people, especially well-meaning LDS members, are very afraid of repenting. This seems to be because it comes with a stigma. Most of us seem to think that repentance is only for people who have failed. But, as we talked about in the last chapter, that is wrong. Repentance isn't for those who fail; it's for those who love God.

Through the simple yet significant act of repentance we accomplish several things: we proclaim our faith in Christ, we conquer our fear of men, we experience the opportunity of a second chance. Most important though, we reclaim our relationship with God. Basically when we repent we are saying, "I made a choice that took me further away from you, Lord. I miss you. I want to be close to you. I'm not going to make that choice again."

Repentance truly is the intersection of faith and fear. Either we believe Christ and His offering to us and lay claim to it through repentance and faith, or we falter, becoming a victim to our fear of men. In the Book of Mormon Alma the Younger directed his priests, "Yea, even he commanded them that they should preach nothing save it were repentance and faith on the Lord, who had redeemed his people" (Mosiah 18:20). He knew that no other act demonstrates our faith and love for God more simply and powerfully than the act of repentance. It is a brave expression that allows us to be in the now and avoid the wastelands of past regrets and future anxieties.

I also talked previously about the difference between guilt and shame. That difference bears repeating here simply because shame is the root of the fear of repentance. It is shame that keeps us from feeling God's love and turning back to Him. Guilt, however, will make our senses keen to the loss of God's presence that we are feeling. It will motivate us to change. It is important to note that guilt can come from things we have done and things that have happened to us. But guilt was never meant to be a stopping place. The minute we stop and wallow in it, we turn it into shame and open ourselves up to unproductive behaviors. As it was emphasized earlier, when it comes to guilt from sin, we need to remember there really are only two kinds of sin: sins we have repented for and sins we have not yet repented for.

Once we repent, all that guilt disappears. Sometimes we don't feel it disappear all at once, but it does go away. And in its place is the joy of God's love. Speaking of his own transformation from fear of repentance to the joy of God's love, Alma the Younger said this, "My soul hath been redeemed from the gall of bitterness and bonds of iniquity. I was in the darkest abyss; but now I behold the marvelous light of God. My soul was racked with eternal torment; but I am snatched, and my soul is pained no more" (Mosiah 27:29). We too can be moved from soul-wrenching pain to marvelous light.

Don't let fear of repentance or shame hold you back from experiencing God's love.

Veil Number Three: Fear of Inadequacy versus Love of Christ

Another major reason we hold ourselves back is the fear of inadequacy. So many of us have a simple, straightforward case of the Not-Good-Enoughs. We aren't good enough to be the Primary president. We aren't good enough parents to our children. We aren't good enough at our jobs. We aren't good enough at reading our scriptures. We are good enough at . . . well, pretty much everything.

I've touched on this earlier in the book but it is worth considering here again because this fear is a particularly paralyzing catch-22. We either don't try and fail or we try and fail anyway because *good enough* is an ever-moving target. This fear truly works like a veil because it blankets our minds and filters everything we see through its vague fabric. After all, it isn't that you aren't good. It's that you aren't good *enough.* Good isn't hard to be. All of us can be good. But good enough? That's another story.

Think about it this way. I can make a pretty good cake. But is it good *enough* to win a prize? Probably not. Maybe you can paint a pretty good picture. But is it good *enough* to charge people money to see it? Again, probably not.

Now, most of us are probably savvy enough to realize that a cake or a painting can still be enjoyed even if it isn't prize winning. However, we almost never apply this logic to ourselves. Maybe you held a pretty good family home evening. But was it good enough to save your children's souls? Probably not. Maybe you were pretty good about saying your prayers every morning and night. But was it good enough to keep you sin free? Definitely not.

Here's why this veil is so insidious: because it is partially true. Most of our other fears are basically false. If you look at them skeptically enough, you can see how they don't hold up. But not with inadequacy. The truth is that you, no matter how hard you try, no matter how much work you do, no matter how much you learn and improve, will never be good enough. Never. In fact, you won't even get close. That much is a true.

But, just like not getting a prize for your cake doesn't mean it is a terrible cake, your life is not a zero-sum game. It isn't all or nothing. This fear is only partially true. Your life and your efforts do count for something but not like you think. They will never add up to enough to tip the scales of eternity in your favor, but that's because they aren't supposed to.

Just like pushing through your fear of repentance brings God's love into your life, when you let go of your fear of inadequacy, when you just accept that you alone are not enough, the healing of Christ's gospel can come rushing in. Because that is the whole truth: you are never good enough but you and Christ together are always more than good enough. You were never meant to save your children's souls or keep yourself sin free. You were meant to engage in behavior like family home evening and personal prayer in order to show Christ your willingness to be saved through His Atonement, and then He makes your efforts enough. With Christ on your team you will always hit your mark because His atoning sacrifice fills in any and all gaps, and our imperfections leave.

When speaking of his own fear of inadequacy, Elder Quentin L. Cook put it this way: "It is our faith in Jesus Christ that sustains us at the crossroads of life's journey. It is the first principle of the gospel. Without it we will spin our wheels at the intersection, spending our precious time but getting nowhere. It is Christ who offers the invitation to follow Him, to give Him our burden, and to carry His yoke, 'for [His] yoke is easy, and [His] burden is light' (Matthew 11:30). . . . When we choose to follow Christ in faith rather than choosing another path out of fear, we are blessed with a consequence that is consistent with our choice (see D&C 6:34–36)."[1]

When we focus on making our love for Christ a reality through our actions, we can let go of our inadequacies and fears, making way for more of His love to come into our lives.

True Love Always Wins

It's cheesy but true: true love does always win. I've seen it in my clients when parents bring in a troubled son and by listening lovingly and encouraging him, change comes. I've seen it in couples on the brink of divorce who learn to set aside the pain they've caused each other and lean on forgiveness and new, kinder behaviors. I've seen it in people with depression and anxiety who learn to love themselves, flaws and all.

In each and every case, it is because they have learned to push through their fears by choosing love: loving their lives and the experiences that happen to them, feeling Heavenly Father's love for them, feeling Christ's love, and then sharing that love.

Jesus Christ told His disciples, "Greater love hath no man than this, that a man lay down his life for his friends" (John 15:13). In that simple statement He not only explained what His ultimate sacrifice would entail but also laid out a path for you and me. If we love our families, our God, and ourselves we will lay our lives down in faith, not fear. True love is faith-centered love. It helps you choose to do the things that will enable you with the power you need to push through your fears and become better, moment by moment, right now.

Note

1. Quentin L. Cook, "Live by Faith and Not by Fear," *Ensign*, November 2007, 73.

Chapter 11
Be Connected, Feel Safe, Love

Dave was entering a new phase of life. It was clear to everyone but him. His wife still had the divorce papers, and he was still only seeing his kids occasionally and so he, understandably, still felt stuck. But so many things about him had changed. He was taking better care of himself, eating better, getting more sleep. He was holding his head up higher and making eye contact more often. He was more relaxed, there was a lot less tension in his face and jaw. I was very excited about Dave seeing it in himself.

As we talked during our session, he talked about how the Fearless Moral Inventory affected him. After we had completed it (it took a couple sessions to get it done) he took it home but left it in his car. He couldn't bring himself to have it in the apartment. However, one day after work he decided it was easier to keep it in the house somewhere than look at it every day in the car.

He read it, and, even though it took some work, he tried to avoid judging himself for his fears and mistakes. He had screwed up, more than once, but he was trying to do better, and that mattered.

"I don't know, James, it seems kinda silly but I keep telling myself that judgment is God's, and so I just need to stop judging myself and just try to do better."

"That doesn't sound silly to me. It sounds healthy."

Dave chuckled. "Well, it's certainly different for me! It's still hard, though. I feel so alone. Most nights in the apartment I'm just, well, alone. I sit there with nothing but work and more work."

"Pretty lonely, huh?"

"Ugh. I hate that word. Lonely. *It sounds so, I don't know, adolescent. I mean, it's not like I'm some teenager afraid to ask the pretty girl out on a*

date. I'm a grown man with a job and kids and a wife. A wife who won't talk to me, but still."

"True. You aren't a teenager, but in some ways this separation and possible divorce have set you back a few years." I needed to tread lightly. Dave seemed on the verge of an important insight, but he was also prone to pulling back when he felt threatened.

"James, I thought therapy was supposed to make me feel good! That sure didn't!" He chuckled ruefully.

"I'm making you feel good in the long run. Moment to moment I make no promises." We were still doing okay, but the lightbulb wasn't turning on yet.

"I don't know. I guess, yeah, I am lonely. But, again, James, I'm a grown man. It's not like I can go to Boy Scouts and make new friends."

"Church is a good place to start. Can you make friends there?"

"We're men, James. We don't have friends. We have basketball buddies and home teaching companions but not friends."

"I think you know that's a ridiculous stereotype, Dave. Why don't you go to basketball at the church?"

"I'm just not into that I guess."

"What are you into?"

"I really don't know. I mean, for so long all I did was work and fight with my wife. And, well, look at porn. I don't have hobbies."

I looked him right in the eye and raised my eyebrows.

"What? James, am I supposed to be getting something? What is it this time?"

"You don't have any hobbies? You don't know what you like to do? I think it's pretty clear where you need to start, then."

"Huh?"

"Who you need to become friends with first."

Still puzzled, Dave slowly shook his head for a moment. Then he put his face in his hands and started chuckling ruefully again. "You mean me, don't you? I need to get to know myself better, right? So help me, James, if you say I need to start dating myself I'm walking out of here right now."

"Don't worry, Dave; I only use that line with my female clients. But, yes, you do need to get to know yourself better. You need to reconnect with you."

"You still sound like Oprah," he groaned. "But fine. Where do we start?"

Admittedly, Carolyn wasn't the easiest person to get to know. She herself told me in our first session that she wasn't the kind of person who made small talk. "I'm a get-down-to-business kind of gal." This made Carolyn a force to be reckoned with when it came to getting things done and running her business effectively. But it didn't always make her relationships easy. This hadn't bothered Carolyn too much until she had started to slow down and breathe more. In those quiet moments she realized that while she loved her husband and children very much, she really didn't know them all that well.

"It was a bit disheartening, James. They were all sitting there watching a movie and laughing, and I was in the kitchen washing dishes and making my list of things to get done the next day—it was Saturday so the list was full of errands and chores—and it hit me: I can't even tell you my kids' favorite colors. I know what grade they are getting in every subject, and I can tell you every song they learned on the piano this last year, but I have no idea who they are. The same goes for my husband. Which really makes me sad. I mean, we got married because we loved each other, and part of why I loved him was I felt like he was so easy-going and such an open book. I felt like I knew him on a deep level, in a way I didn't know anyone else. I certainly don't feel that way now."

My first inclination was to ask Carolyn what she was going to do about that feeling but it seemed more productive to let her sit with the feeling for a bit.

"You said it's 'disheartening.' What do you mean by that? What are you really feeling?"

She pursed her lips and sighed. She reacted to my "What are you feeling?" questions about as well as Dave did. It wasn't her favorite thing to think about.

"Sad, I guess. And maybe a little lost too. I mean, I tell myself I'm doing all this for them, but if I don't even know them, can I really say that?" She sighed again and collapsed back in her chair, abandoning her usually straight posture. "I guess you could say what I felt while I was washing those dishes was lonely.*"*

"That's a hard feeling. What did you do that night, while they were watching the movie?"

"Finished the dishes as fast as I could and joined them in front of the movie. There wasn't much of it left, but I got to hang out for about twenty minutes."

"Nice! Did your kids or husband say anything?"

She blushed and rolled her eyes. "My youngest said, 'Mom! What are you doing here? You're too busy to be here!"

"Out of the mouths of babes, huh?"

"Yeah. I've got some work to do, don't I?"

I nodded. "But don't worry. This will be much easier than the other work you've done. This is all about fun. You're going to start connecting with your kids and husband through good times."

Connection: Finding Safety in an Unsafe World

One evening in a counseling session I asked a couple who was struggling with financial differences to create a budget together. I gave them an outline of a budget and told them they had fifteen minutes to work it out while I left the room.

When I returned to my office, I asked them if they had completed the budget, and they said yes. As they handed me their budget I briefly reviewed it and then set the budget aside. I told them this had very little to do with creating a budget and more to do with how safe they had kept each other while working through a difficult situation.

I asked, "As you worked on the budget, did you listen respectfully to each other? Did you validate each other's ideas? Were you patient with each other? Did you try to find win-win solutions to the problems instead of just promoting your own agendas?" I then asked them to grade each other (A, B, C, D, or F) with regards to how safe they made each other feel while working on the budget together. Sadly, they gave each other a D.

Often it is not a particular issue in our lives (like creating a budget), which creates anxiety and worry, that ruins our relationships. It is the *process* that we have been using that has created a feeling of fear, distrust, anxiety, and contempt for one another. Most of the processes we've been taught, especially if we come from high-conflict homes or have been in high-conflict marriages, are ones that teach us to win by promoting our own ideas rather than win by keeping ourselves and the people we value safe.

Anything is obtainable if we can remember to keep each other feeling safe and loved while we work on hard issues. It is hard to expect two people to want to be around each other if they are constantly making each other feel unsafe through words, actions, and attitudes. Unless we can learn how to love each other and keep each other safe, we will not experience one of the greatest human feelings of being connected with another person.

Just like perfect love can cast out fear, it can also cast out stress and distrust. But in order for us to have that kind of love in our lives we need to be able to connect to the sources of love in our lives. So many of us today cannot. I would say that is, perhaps, the primary reason people end up in my office. They have lost the ability to connect to who matters most in their lives.

This couple I mentioned was not unique. Our modern lives and attitudes often set us up to be disconnected from the things and people that matter most. Remember everything I've said about distraction? Every time we are distracted we are not connected. Distraction is the opposite of connection so it makes sense that the single best way to fight distraction is through connection.

It is only through relationships that we can learn to love and be loved. It is only through relationships that we can learn to be safe.

The Science of Connection

Connection is a basic human need. Without connections to the world around us, we fall apart psychologically and physically. Many of us are familiar with stories of orphans in Eastern European countries having severe emotional troubles and, in some cases, even dying from a lack of love. In their book, *Born for Love*, psychiatrists Bruce D. Perry and Maria Szalavitz explain that a lack of affection can actually cause death. "When an infant falls below the threshold of physical affection needed to stimulate the production of growth hormone and the immune system, his body starts shutting down."[1]

Most of us may not run the risk of dying from a lack of love, but we do run the risk of negatively impacting our health. There is a very real tie between the quality of our relationships and our health. Low-quality relationships lead to a low quality of life.

One way psychologists have studied connection over the years is through what is known as *attachment theory*. Basically this looks at how safe people feel in their connection to the most important people in their lives. Most attachment theory focuses on babies and their parents, but the patterns that emerge during those early years are proven to affect us as adults also.

Essentially what they've found is that people tend to form connections in four basic ways: secure, avoidant, ambivalent, or disorganized. If you are avoidant, ambivalent, or disorganized in your attachment style you are more likely to struggle in your relationships. By avoiding relationships, not caring about relationships, or not prioritizing your relationships properly the belief that relationships are fundamentally unsafe is confirmed, and the conviction that our needs will never be met through relationships is solidified. Shallow connections and isolation are the result. This can also impact your health because it can create anxiety, depression, and other health problems.

One famous study looked at over nine hundred centenarians in Okinawa for more than thirty years and found that one of the best indicators of good health and disease survivability was how many social connections an individual had. If a person had few social connections they were more likely to die before old age. If they felt they had a solid social safety net, they were not only more likely to live longer lives but they also had better disease survivability and experienced a higher quality of life because they had lower rates or dementia and depression.[2]

To put it more simply: we were designed as humans to be safely connected to the people around us. This doesn't mean that we all have to have enough friends to win a popularity contest, but it does mean that we need to spend time and energy building secure and safe connections with those around us.

Think about when you feel safest—most secure. Is it when you are wrapped up in a blanket reading a good book or watching a movie, giving you the feeling others are present with you? Is it when you are with your children or your family? Think about the last time you got a hug from someone you trusted. That relaxed feeling that washed through your body? That's attachment at work.

The Spiritual Basis of Connection

Of course, we are not just physical beings. As Latter-day Saints we are fond of saying we are spiritual beings having a mortal journey. That is nowhere more true than it is in the context of connection. God designed this life to revolve around connections. He means for us to interact with, rely on, and relate to the people around us.

In His earthly ministry, Christ himself emphasized that human relationships and connections with each other are equal in value to our relationship with Him, saying "Inasmuch as ye did it not to one of the least of these, ye did it not to me" (Matthew 25:45). On another occasion He taught, "Therefore if thou bring thy gift to the altar, and there rememberest that thy brother hath ought against thee; Leave there thy gift before the altar, and go thy way; first be reconciled to thy brother, and then come and offer thy gift" (Matthew 5:23-24). This connection between our relationships to others and our relationships with our Lord are direct ones. The better we are connecting with others in Christlike ways, the better we will be at connecting with Christ. And the better we are at connecting with Christ, the better we will be at connecting with others.

One reason this is true is it's through experiencing loving relationships with each other that we are able to understand His love for us. Christ was, and is, aware that we cannot have a connection with Him while being in conflict with our fellow man. Not only is it contrary to the gospel He taught, but it also makes it impossible to build the kingdom of God on earth if there is enmity between people. Christ makes it very clear, "If you are not one, you are not mine" (D&C 38:27).

The most dire sins, those with the worst consequences, are those that harm the connections between our spirit brothers and sisters and ourselves. The worst thing God can do to a person is what happened to Satan in premortality; be cast out. By insisting on rebelling against Father, Lucifer set himself up to be forever separate and alone. Our theology teaches us that hell is not a never-ending ring of flames. Rather, it is an outer darkness, an eternal loneliness, that forever severs the sinner from their families and their Lord.

Think about all the ways our Father in Heaven organizes His work on earth. We are set up in wards and stakes and assigned to minister to each other. We are commanded to gather together every seven days to worship and, at least once a month, share our deepest convictions and experiences. We are told over and over that the most basic unit of heaven is the family. Everywhere you look, Father is pushing us to connect with the people around us. It is the single best way to help us become more like Him. After all, He is the ultimate connection: a loving parent who has known us and will love us for eternity.

Three Essential Connections

If connection is so important that a lack of it can harm our health and kill our spirits, then what do we do when we find ourselves struggling with our connections? If relationships are of paramount importance, how do we build stronger ones? Over the years I've found that it is easiest for people to break down their connections into three basic groups and pick one way to shore up those connections.

Typically we think of connection as one kind of relationship: the connection with others around us. That is an important connection, but you actually need to build two other connections first. Connection happens on three dependent levels: with ourselves, with God, and with others. Without the first, you cannot have the second and the third. This doesn't mean you have to perfect each level of connection before you move on to the next. None of us will ever be perfect, and I talked about embracing failure a couple of chapters ago, so what is most important is that you build a bit on each level continuously.

Let me break each one down so you can see how best to start increasing your connections.

Connecting with Ourselves

Most people react to this idea very much like Dave did. Not many are excited about the idea of "dating" themselves. It sounds like such a poor substitute for a truly pleasurable activity. It's like eating something that is chocolate-y flavored instead of actual chocolate. It's close but not quite.

However, connecting with yourself doesn't have to be that way. The point isn't to say, "I can go to a movie by myself and enjoy it just as much as I would with a date. I'm not ashamed to be in public alone!" The point is to get to know yourself with the same focus as you do when you start dating someone.

For example, let's go back to someone like Dave. He's probably fine with going to movies alone and eating dinner alone. He doesn't really mind going out and buying something nice for himself. The real problem is that he doesn't actually know what kind of movie he likes. He doesn't know what to order for dinner. He's not sure what he would buy for himself, given the money and the opportunity.

Most of us lack this kind of knowledge about ourselves. It's a byproduct of our very busy, distracted, and, yes, disconnected lives. Between work and family and church and who knows what else, we can hardly be bothered to notice the color of the flowers on the side of the road, much less our own preferences.

This lack of self-knowledge goes even deeper, though. After all, given a little time and some pressure most people can figure out the details mentioned above. However, what they don't know are the whys and the whats of their lives. Why do they like the things they do? What are they truly passionate about? What convictions caused them to make their biggest commitments? What weaknesses caused them to make their biggest mistakes? Why did they choose the current path their life is on? What are they willing to do to create the life they want?

The easiest way to answer these questions is to work on being present in the now. After all, most of our distractions aren't just cell phones but rather the shame we carry regarding our past mistakes and the anxiety we project onto the future. If we can focus on the now space by paying attention to ourselves and our reactions, then the shame and the anxiety disappear.

All of the ways I've talked about being present and aware in the previous chapters will help, but when it comes to connecting with yourself there is one big thing you have to do. And, yes, this has a little bit of an Oprah-esque ring to it, but it is necessary. You have to start engaging in self-care.

What Is Self-Care?

Self-care is a term that gets bandied about a lot these days, and many people invoke it incorrectly. So what is it exactly? Well, self-care is not an excuse for bad behavior, bailing on commitments, or staying in your comfort zone. Rather self-care is pausing to listen to yourself to find out what you really need and then meeting that need.

Still sound a little fuzzy? Here's an example:

Let's say you're a highly anxious person. Self-care for you might look like passing on certain social opportunities because they would be too agitating for you to truly connect with the people around you. Self-care, however, is *not* skipping out on all social opportunities because that would be detrimental in the long run by isolating you.

That's the true definition of self-care: something that meets a need you are having right now, without making you sacrifice your long-term needs, goals, or desires. If an act sabotages the big picture of your life, it is not self-care.

Some other examples:

Self-care is making your favorite casserole because you had a long day and need something nourishing; self-care is not eating the entire thing in front of the TV.

Self-care is taking a nap because you are tired; self-care is not spending an entire weekend in bed (unless you have the flu!).

Self-care is talking out your problems with a friend; self-care is not gossip or dredging up old problems.

Are you starting to see the difference?

The trick with self care is that is cannot be a reaction. It has to be an independent and informed action that addresses what your mind is needing. Long stressful day? The base reaction might be to yell at your spouse and eat an entire container of ice cream when you get home. The independent and informed action is to tell your spouse you had a bad day, ask for some space, dish up enough ice cream that you can enjoy it but not over-indulge, then sit down and eat and think of nothing but the creamy deliciousness on your spoon.

Self-care starts with asking yourself what you need, listening for the honest answer, then providing that for yourself.

Connecting with God

If connecting with yourself is all about listening to yourself, connecting with God is all about listening to Him through the Holy Ghost. It's a process we talk about in church all the time. I'm sure we could all rattle off a ready list of answers: prayer, scripture study, family home evening, temple attendance, ministering—the list goes on. However, we also all probably know that a checklist approach to connecting with God works about as well as a checklist approach when dating. You would never decide to marry someone by simply going through a checklist of activities with them. Why would we think that we can get to know God that way?

The best way to connect with God is to take that list of Sunday School answers and, again, be present with it. Bring those ideas into the present moment. President Uchtdorf put it this way, "We improve our relationship with our Heavenly Father by learning of Him, by communing with Him, by repenting of our sins, and by actively following Jesus Christ. . . . To strengthen our relationship with God, we need some meaningful time alone with Him. Quietly focusing on daily personal prayer and scripture study, always aiming to be worthy of a current temple recommend—these will be some wise investments of our time and efforts to draw closer to our Heavenly Father."[3]

Often we end up trying to cram in our scripture study or our prayers just so we can say we got them done. However, what if when we sat down to read scriptures, we prayed for a moment first and asked Heavenly Father to draw our minds to what we really need? What if before we prayed we asked ourselves what the most important question or request we have for our Father in Heaven is? As we read our scriptures and kneel to pray, what if we stopped and took a deep breath and just asked how that particular piece of scripture was meaningful to us as individuals?

We know that the Holy Ghost is a still, small voice. But sometimes we forget that we have to make ourselves still and small too in order to hear it. Take a moment to prepare yourself before you pray. Take a deep breath. Clear your mind of all the voices and judgments pin-balling around in there. Close your eyes, and imagine God's love pouring over you. Then, pray. Then open your scriptures.

Another exercise to try to increase your connection with God is to remember a time that you felt His love, whether it was for a moment, an hour, or a day. Do your best to remember what that moment sounded like, smelled like, felt like. As you do, God's love will start to become real inside you again. Try to do nothing but feel that love for two minutes. It doesn't seem like something that would be hard to do, but in real life it is actually quite hard. When those voices in your head start telling you that it wasn't real or that you didn't deserve it, let them go, imagine them sailing out of your mind, and go back to focusing on that feeling. As you get better at it, extend the time. Work up to ten minutes of just remembering and feeling God's love for you. There is no better antidote to shame and anxiety than God's love.

Learning to be vulnerable and safe with someone is one of the hardest things we will learn to do, and it isn't necessarily easy to do with God either. God asks that we bring Him what scripture calls a *circumcised heart*. In Romans 2:29, it is described this way, "And circumcision is that of the heart, in the spirit, and not in the letter; whose praise is not of men, but of God." This is one of the most vivid images in scripture. God is asking us to remove the flesh, the muscle, and the bone, and allow Him direct access to the most vital organ in our body. The circumcised heart is symbolic of becoming emotionally and spiritually nude with Him so He can show us, through His Son and through His spirit, how to grow and become like Him. He is aware that there will be skinned knees and broken hearts along the way but He promises to give us peace through the journey if we will give Him our heart. It is through transparency and vulnerability with God that we will know what it means to be truly loved and have our deepest needs met through our relationship with Him and others.

President Eyring once gave a talk telling about how he took time to write down every day how he felt God's love in his life. He described the benefits this way:

> Before I would write, I would ponder this question: 'Have I seen the hand of God reaching out to touch us or our children or our family today?' As I kept at it, something began to happen. As I would cast my mind over the day, I would see evidence of what God had done for one of us that I had not recognized in the busy moments of the day. As that happened, and it happened often, I realized that trying to remember

> had allowed God to show me what He had done. . . . More than gratitude began to grow in my heart. Testimony grew. I became ever more certain that our Heavenly Father hears and answers prayers. I felt more gratitude for the softening and refining that come because of the Atonement of the Savior Jesus Christ. And I grew more confident that the Holy Ghost can bring all things to our remembrance—even things we did not notice or pay attention to when they happened.[4]

What President Eyring described was basically the circumcising of his heart to build a secure attachment to our Heavenly Father. Just like we need secure attachments to our earthly family in order to feel safe and loved, we need a secure attachment to our Heavenly Father to feel safe and loved. Heavenly Father's love is there for us, every moment of every day. That connection alone can do much to wipe away fear, anxiety, shame, worry, and stress. All we have to do is notice it.

Connecting with Others

God told Adam in the Garden of Eden that it wasn't good for people to be alone. That was why, in part, Eve was created. God organized this world in families because He knew we needed to be connected to each other to be healthy. But relationships with others are some of the hardest things we will do in our lives.

The famous philosopher Arthur Schopenhauer wrote in his *Parerga und Paralipomena*, Volume I, Chapter XXXI, Section 396 that human relationships very much resemble porcupine relationships. Basically what he said is that porcupines have the need to be warm and the best way to meet that need is to huddle close together. Unfortunately, when they get too close, they poke each other with their quills, which pushes them away from each other. For porcupines to be comfortable, there is a constant shifting between too far and too close.

In human relationships it is very similar. We all have the need to experience the warmth of close relationships with others, but often when we get too close our weaknesses and quirks quickly turn into annoyances, and alienation occurs. Many times this alienation happens in ways that feel entirely unsafe to us. We yell or say cutting remarks. We shut down and emotionally freeze out our loved ones. We lash out in anger and do or say deeply hurtful things. All of which makes it that much harder to be connected the next time around. But our need for the warmth of connection propels us back together, regardless of how safe we feel.

Unfortunately, until we can learn to be vulnerable and safe with each other we will feel fearful of one another, and we will become emotionally under-nourished. Often people will find themselves in a cycle where, due to past painful events in their life, they have convinced themselves that vulnerability and transparency are bad. But, if we don't learn how to be transparent and safe with other people, we will continue to exist on emotional scraps from unhealthy sources. We see through the internet how people attempt to create cyber connections; giving themselves the illusion of connection but with no flesh and blood present. It is easy to fool myself in thinking I am connected to others when in reality I am just trying to keep myself safe from the potential pain of real relationships.

In our society we see people who are trying to become totally self-sufficient to the extent that they won't have to rely on anyone else. We often call these people survivalists. Fundamentally, they see others around them as enemies, and they are convinced the key to surviving is to be totally self-sufficient. And, do whatever it takes to protect what is theirs. In truth, the way people survive through the difficult times of life, whether physically or emotionally, is through their connection with others. During the difficult times, they have a network that they could rely on for physical, emotional, and spiritual support when things get hard. They recognize that investing in a healthy network of friends and associates creates stability and insulates them from the debilitating effects of isolation and hopelessness. It is through connection we typically discover our best self as we rely on and support those around us.

While working with a father and his two sons in counseling I would often discuss what it means to be safe and loved with each other. This family had a long history of hurting each other and being hurt. One day during a counseling session, I told the family we were going to a place that sold rocks. When we arrived, I asked the family to find a sizable rock they all liked, one that could be carried by each of them. After about fifteen minutes they found their rock. Curious, they asked what it was for. I told them they would have to give it to me and wait and see.

Two weeks later I met with the family and gave them their rock. Etched on the rock were the words "Safe & Loved." I explained to the family that this was their new mantra. The goal in every interaction they had was to keep each other feeling safe and let each other know they are loved. I had each family member trace the words on the rock with their finger. Each week as I worked with this family teaching them how to keep each other feeling safe and loved while working on issues, they slowly began to understand that even in the hardest of moments it was still possible to keep each other safe and feel love. Through time and practice this family began to experience what it meant to feel safe and loved with each other. Instead of seeing each other as an adversary or a competitor, they began to see each other as a supporter and teammate.

This is often easier said than done, but it also isn't as hard as you might think it would be. The first step is simple. And just as we needed to with all the other connection types, we need to do a lot of listening here too.

As families, friends, or couples, sit down and begin to define what it means to feel safe and loved and connected with each other. Have each person write on a piece of paper the words that make them feel safe and loved, the actions that make them feel safe and loved, and the body language that makes them feel safe and loved. Make an agreement with one another that you will not engage in making the other person feel unsafe even in a setting where there is conflict with each other. Ban expressions in your conversations such as, "you always" and "you never." Figure out which words put you on the defensive, and let your partner know to avoid them, and be sure to avoid theirs. Talk about how "we" can work together to figure out the conflict. Make the effort to listen first (remember, be a contributor before you become an editor) and counsel second. Above all, make sure that everyone feeling safe and loved now is the cornerstone of your relationships.

The Positive Cycle of Connection

The truth is that each type of connection and attachment helps foster the others. So the more we connect to God, the more we are able to connect to others. If we are connecting to others in a healthy way, we will learn more about ourselves. The more we know about ourselves, the better we can connect with God. And so it goes. Of course, deeply connecting isn't easy. It takes time and patience and effort. However, the effort is worth it. Connections drive growth and happiness. As stated earlier from the Doctrine and Covenants, we are cautioned, "If ye are not one, ye are not mine" (38:27). By being one, by being connected, we become His, and we are able to enter into His rest.

Notes

1. Maia Szalavitz, "How Orphanages Kill Babies—and Why No Child under 5 Should Be in One," The Huffington Post, November 17, 2011, accessed September 03, 2018, http://www.huffingtonpost.com/maia-szalavitz/how-orphanages-kill-babie_b_549608.html.
2. Bradley J. Willcox, D. Craig Willcox, and Makoto Suzuki, *The Okinawa Program: How the Worlds Longest-lived People Achieve Everlasting Health—and How You Can Too* (New York: Three Rivers Press, 2002).
3. Dieter F. Uchtdorf, "Of Things That Matter Most," *Ensign*, November 2010, 21.
4. Henry B. Eyring, "O Remember, Remember," *Ensign*, November 2007, 67.

Chapter 12
Be Renewed through Creation

One of Lana's greatest fears was, in all truth, dancing. She was so afraid of doing it that she wouldn't even dance with her kids in the kitchen. Her littlest was still in the princess phase of life and was always singing some song or another and begging Mommy to dance with her. Lana was so afraid she couldn't even join her daughter in a few moments of pretend.

"It's this body, James. Maybe years ago, if I hadn't quit when I was a kid, I could have been a better dancer, but not now. I'm too old. Too flabby. I've had three kids. Nobody wants to see me dance."

"Except those three kids you gave birth to. And, really, they don't want to see you dance. They just want you to have fun with them. Is there something so wrong with your body that you can't do that?"

As per her usual, Lana had a story about her ex-husband and how he made fun of her for dancing. She also had stories about her dance foibles as a child: her teachers had told her she wasn't any good, she had tripped on stage, the list went on.

"But we've got a real problem now," she continued. "For Activity Days, the girls are supposed to participate in a Mommy-Daughter talent show, and they want to dance. I've tried talking them out of it but, James, they won't agree to anything else. So now I either have to make a fool of myself or risk letting my kids down."

"All right, Lana, I'm gonna tell you to take a breather from the high-stakes thinking. The situation isn't really that dire."

She started to stew. "Well, maybe it doesn't sound like it to you, but it feels *like it is."*

"Fair enough," I countered, "but this also sounds like a tremendous opportunity. You've got the chance to create not only a dance with your daughters but a tremendous memory. I think this squarely falls into your Year of Yes category."

She put her head down on the table. "I was afraid you were going to say that."

As the weeks passed, Lana ended up with more and more opportunities to dance. Not only with her kids but also with some other single moms she was getting to know. They all took a Zumba class together at the rec center, and Lana had to say yes. Slowly but surely, over time, it got less torturous. As the day drew nearer and nearer to the Activity Days talent show, Lana was letting the spirit of her Year of Yes take over. She and her girls choreographed a silly dance to a medley of songs from Disney movies. They even created matching costumes to wear that night.

After the event, at our next session, I asked her how she felt about it.

"It was so ridiculous, James. So *ridiculous. But it was worth it. I mean, the performance was kind of messy. Ava forgot her part so she just ran around the stage in circles, and Evaline tore her costume taking a bow, but overall it was fun. I think my favorite part, though, honestly, was not the performance. It was making up the dance. And the costumes. That was fun. It was so nice to just, I don't know, make something. I could just focus on the costumes and not worry about work or kids or bad memories or the bills that were due next week. I could just be."*

"It sounds like you need more of that in your life, Lana. You need more time to create things—especially good days. Those are the best creations."

Dave's wife had finally filed the divorce papers.

"I knew it was coming, James. I really did. But, at the same time, I didn't. I guess mostly I was just trying not to think about it. I think I was hoping we could just stay in limbo forever. Being separated wasn't that bad. We could have made it work."

Tears threatened to spill, and Dave stopped talking. Maybe if he stopped talking he'd stop feeling too.

"Dave, I'm really sorry about this. This is definitely hard news."

"Yeah, but who can blame her? If I were in her shoes, I would have done the same things. I'm not marriage material. I'm too broken. I've got so many

problems. Why would anyone want to be with me? My own kids don't even like me." The tears did spill out now.

"Dave," I began, "I know it feels like you're losing everything, but I promise you aren't."

"Those are very easy words for you to say from your side of the table, James. You have no idea what I'm losing."

"I may not know exactly what it feels like, Dave, but I do know how much I love my wife and kids and how bad it feels when I let them down. I've also seen a lot of other men go through this. I'm not going to lie, the next year or eighteen months is going to be hard. They'll probably be the hardest of your life. But if you do it right, this hard time is also a huge opportunity, Dave."

He snorted derisively. "Again, easy for you to say."

"You've spent the last twelve years creating a life you didn't want. The consequences of your choices are hard but, Dave, think about everything you've done since you and your wife separated. You aren't the same guy. You can now create the life you want."

Dave didn't say anything and wouldn't even look at me.

"This really sucks today, and it is probably going to suck for a while longer, Dave, but I can promise you that no matter what you've done, no matter where you've been, God has good things in store for the people that let Him bless their lives. Let God guide you. You'll get through this. You've got more power than you know."

Shaking Off the Dust of Life

My kids' grade school art teacher had a poster on her desk that I loved. The border was painted to look like a garden with mystical creatures in it, and in the middle it said, "Earth without art is just *eh*." It was a great statement, and I knew she'd be a great teacher because it was 100 percent true. Without art, and the other creative enterprises we all engage in, life is just . . . *eh*.

We all know that life is full of troubling things. Difficulties and stressors and worries and anxieties all around. There are very few days in our lives when we make it from sunup to sundown without some problem cropping up. However, there are also very few days in our lives when we don't make it from sunup to sundown without the opportunity to create something amazing. Another quote I love is attributed to Pablo Picasso (but who knows who actually said it), and it says, "Art washes from the soul the dust of everyday life." It's those moments of creation that take the stress out of life and make it all worthwhile.

Now, I know most of you are probably arguing with me in your heads right now. You might be saying something along the lines of, "I'm not an artist/writer/musician. I'm not a creative type!" But guess what. You *are* creative. We all are. It's part of what our brains are wired for. In his 1939 essay "On Fairy Stories," J. R. R. Tolkien says,

> Although now long estranged,
> Man is not wholly lost nor wholly changed.
> Dis-graced he may be, yet is not de-throned,
> and keeps the rags of lordship once he owned:
> Man, Sub-creator, the refracted Light
> through whom is splintered from a single White
> to many hues, and endlessly combined
> in living shapes that move from mind to mind.
> Though all the crannies of the world we filled
> with Elves and Goblins, though we dared to build
> Gods and their houses out of dark and light,
> and sowed the seed of dragons—'twas our right
> (used or misused). That right has not decayed:
> we make still by the law in which we're made.[1]

Myths about Creativity

The neuroscience of creativity is still a budding area of research. There is so much that we don't know. But some things we do know: creativity is good for us, and it is something all humans can engage in.

Here are some myths you can let go of. Back in the early 1980s, when brain science was still very new, people were fond of saying you were either right brained or left brained, with the right side being the creative side and the left brain being the logical side. It was thought that you had a dominant side, and that drove the way you were in the world. However, we now know that it takes both sides of the brain to do logical and analytical tasks, and it takes both sides of the brain to do expressive, creative tasks. There is no such thing as left brained or right brained.

In fact, a 2011 study published in the *Journal of Social Psychological and Personality Science* demonstrated that people who engaged in activities that they found interesting enjoyed a host of benefits. It positively affected their cognitive and emotional states (meaning they got smarter and happier) while helping them learn important skills like emotional self-regulation, sustained effort, and long-term attention. Engaging in creative outlets is good for you on emotional, intellectual, and physical levels.[2]

Now, again, I can hear some of you arguing with me because that study talked about doing things that interest you, and that isn't the same as creativity. Well, I'm going to tell you, you are wrong because that is another myth about creativity. So many of us believe that to be creative you have to paint or write songs or poetry. Those are all parts of being creative, but they aren't the only way to be creative.

A more true definition of creativity is *Whenever you create something you are being creative.* This can be cooking dinner (which is sometimes why it is so hard to figure out what to make; it requires creativity!) or decorating your home. It can be going out to the garage and fiddling with the car. It can be carving something or reorganizing a closet. Any activity that requires you to take one set of things and make something new or different out of them is creative.

This brings us to another myth. We often believe that to be creative we have to have something fabulous to show for it at the end. You have to have a perfectly decorated cake or a sculpture you can display in your living room. Again, I'm telling you, that's wrong. Maybe all you created was a car stereo that functions or a bookshelf that no longer resembles the paperback version of the Leaning Tower of Pisa. That is good enough. We often believe that if we don't have something "arty," then it wasn't creative. Not true.

Spiritually Born to Create

Part of why all these myths are just myths is they belie our true identity. Heavenly Father is, first and foremost, a creative being. Yes, He is all powerful, all knowing, and all loving, but what does He use those traits for? Creation. What is the greatest reward you and I can receive in the eternities? The ability to create. Just like we are patterned after our Father physically, we are patterned after Him creatively too. We are literally made to create things.

Because of this, creativity is a spiritual process too. It's something that isn't just nice to engage in but is also necessary for our spiritual growth and development. This is part of why God commanded Adam and Eve to work when they left the Garden of Eden. They needed to make things to learn that they were capable beings and because it tapped into their larger identity as children of God.

President Uchtdorf explained how that fits into our own lives this way, "The desire to create is one of the deepest yearnings of the human soul. No matter our talents, education, backgrounds, or abilities, we each have an inherent wish to create something that did not exist before . . . remember that you are spirit daughters [and sons] of the most creative Being in the universe. . . . We were created with the express purpose and potential of experiencing a fullness of joy. Our birthright—and the purpose of our great voyage on this earth—is to seek and experience eternal happiness. One of the ways we find this is by creating things."[3]

The Spiritual State of Flow

One reason creation is critical to our growth is when we are deeply involved in the creative process we access a part of ourselves that I believe is one of the most tight-knit states of spirit and body working together. This is a state of being where you lose your self-consciousness. All your worries and anxieties disappear. In fact, when you are really in this place time stops and you completely forget yourself. This is the state of flow that I talked about in chapter nine. The easiest way to find flow is to create.

This is because flow is actually a unique state in the brain. It is one area where researchers do understand some of the neuroscience of creativity. When we engage in an activity deeply enough that we find flow, the part of the prefrontal cortex that is responsible for inhibition and self-censorship deactivates. Other parts of the brain become more active. We literally turn off the negative voices in our heads and let the other parts of our brains do what they do best.

I believe that state creates a unique opportunity to commune with our Father in Heaven. Flow is one of the best ways to draw close to Him because as we create we step into His work as the Great Creator of all things. Our mind, our body, our spirit, and our emotions are often operating at peak levels together when we are in the act of creating. So, when we choose to create beauty and light in the world, we will often feel a communion with God we can feel nowhere else. This is a state worth pursuing.

Most often our efforts focus on creating something physical. This is a great place to start. In fact, Elder Marlin K. Jensen said that, "No matter what our life's work turns out to be, I know we'll be happier if we regularly labor with our hands. This can take many forms: yard work, sewing, quilting, cooking, baking, auto repair, home repair—the list is endless and so is the happiness and sense of accomplishment such activities produce."[4]

This is actually a fairly intuitive process, but most of us avoid it because we let the voices in our heads get in the way. Think about when you were little. You probably loved to color, paint, sing, dance, build things with blocks, make up stories. Then, even as an adolescent, you probably played an instrument or dabbled in photography. You maybe did theater or dance or sewing.

So what changed when you were an adult? Why don't you do those things now? Probably because you judged those activities as less valuable and therefore not worth your time or money. However, there's good news too: you can start creating again now, and it's a lot easier than you think.

The Roadmap to Creativity

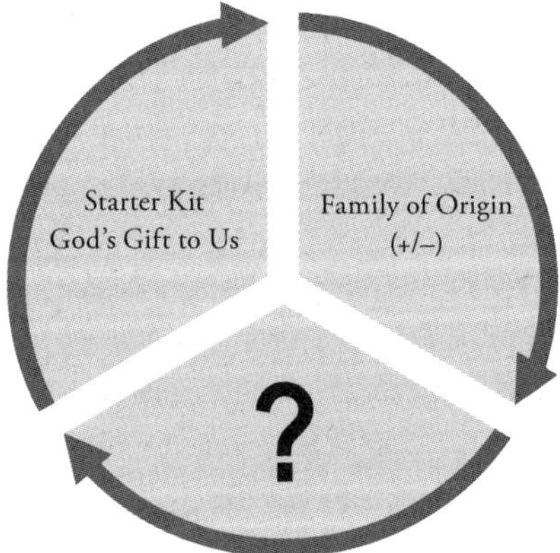

Above is a diagram divided into three parts. In the first part are the words *Starter Kit*. The second part says *Family of Origin*. And the final part is a question mark. These sections each represent a part of your creative inheritance. They are the things you can draw on to start creating.

In the Starter Kit section, I want you to think of your own divine nature. Each one of us came into the world and received some gift(s) from God. In the parable of the talents we read, "And unto one he gave five talents, to another two, and to another one; to every man according to his several ability; and straightway took his journey" (Matthew 25:15). It was God's way of saying, "Here, enjoy this talent while you are on earth." Maybe He gave us an ear for music, or maybe we are good in math, or maybe we have a talent for teaching. Regardless, everyone received some talent upon coming to earth. Think through what you seem to have a knack for or deep enjoyment of. Those things are probably given to you from God to help you create.

In the second part, the Family of Origin section, you should brainstorm all the ways the family you came from was creative. As a member of a family you received some gifts through your genetics and through being taught by your parents. Some of these gifts were positive and some may be negative. These are the skills and abilities that are passed on to us through our families. We often see people praise and blame the things that have been given to them through their families. But for now I want you to just focus on what good things you learned. Generally speaking, families are the best place to learn important skills that will help us in life. So your creative resources from your family could be that you're a good talker or you have the ability to fix things around the house. It could be cooking a great rice pilaf or painting a picture. It doesn't matter what it is—just think of a few things you could have gotten from your family.

In the final part of the diagram we see a question mark. This part is based on your life experiences and feelings. Maybe no one in your family can draw anything beyond a stick figure, but you took art in high school and college and discovered a gift. That's part of your creative resources now. Maybe you went through a difficult time financially and learned to garden to supplement your groceries. That's definitely a creative outlet. Think about what your personal experiences have taught you, and figure out how you can incorporate those into your creative life.

Three Types of Creation

There are three basic types of creative work that we engage in. They are the physical, the metaphysical, and the eternal. All of them are important, and we need to engage mindfully in all of them to help us become what our Heavenly Father intends us to become.

Physical creation is probably the one we are most familiar with. This is painting beautiful pictures, taking eye-popping photographs, sculpting lovely things, writing moving poetry, making decorations for your home, or any other sort of creative activity that ends in something you can see, touch, hear, taste, or smell. This type of creation is fulfilling because we often have something to show for our efforts. This type is also frustrating because if it doesn't go the way we think it should we get discouraged. However, part of the joy of creation is the process. So, the next time you are two hours into a cake that is supposed to look like a pirate chest but barely resembles, well, cake, take a deep breath, step back, and see what you can do. Creativity isn't about the end result. It's about the process.

Metaphysical creation is one that you probably spend time doing but don't realize it. This is when we create things that can't be seen, touched, heard, smelled, or tasted. But even though it doesn't end with something tangible, it is just as important as physical creating. Metaphysical creating is when we intentionally create the feelings, thoughts, and experiences we want to have. This starts by turning off the voices in our heads and learning to be still. This kind of creation starts with us choosing a feeling or relationship or memory that we want to have and then taking action to build that. When we create a positive feeling with another person, we are creating a new good memory with that person. When we find an answer to a problem, we are creating a skill. When we overcome an obstacle, we are creating hope. This kind of creating is more subtle, but when you are mindful and intentional about your experiences, it happens, and it feels great.

The last type of creation I want to talk about is the eternal creation. This is another type of creating that we spend quite a bit of our time doing but don't realize it. Every day, every moment, each of our now moments add up to something bigger than who we are: the eternities. We know that anything we create physically can't be taken with us when we die. What we do get to take into the eternities is our knowledge and our attitudes, the things that have defined us spiritually in this world. We should be intentional about how we create those things too and spend time every day attending to creating more knowledge and cultivating the type of attitude that will serve us well not only here but also in the eternities.

There is one physical thing we do get to take with us into the eternities. There is one thing that we work on making every single day that we can touch, see, and smell. It is our families. All the effort we put into our spouses and children and parents and siblings adds up to creating what will be most valuable to us in the eternities: our relationships.

This is why the now space matters so much. It is the one place where each of us has the power to create something eternal. It is only in the now that we can build relationships. We can't skip forward and build one tomorrow. We can't go back and build one yesterday. It is in each moment that the most important work of building our personal connections gets done.

Eternal Help for Creative Endeavors

If you are still the type of person who thinks that they can't create things or doesn't know where to start, think back to the parable of the talents. It shows us not only how God helps us, but also what the expectation for creation is. In the parable of the talents we see that each person is given at least one talent. Think of it like a starter kit. Then, as the parable goes on, each person makes choices regarding that starter kit, with two of the men using their experience to gain more talents. The only one who doesn't improve on his situation is the one man who doesn't try. He simply buries his starter kit and then makes excuses about why he made the choice that he did.

In this life we are all in a similar situation. Most of us have at least one or two small things we know how to do or can create. We know that Heavenly Father has given gifts of ability to all His children, including you. Maybe it's something small like telling great jokes. Maybe it's something big like stitching beautiful quilts. It really doesn't matter. What matters is what we do with it. We can choose to try to see where our talents take us or we can choose to not try. In the end, it doesn't matter so much what we do or how much progress we've made. What concerns the Lord is that we tried. It is only through trying that we use our now moments the way our Heavenly Father wants us to.

It can also help to remember what the Lord says in Doctrine and Covenants 46:8, "Seek ye earnestly the best gifts, always remembering for what they are given." This scripture is often interpreted as an injunction to keep learning new things and pray for spiritual gifts that we don't yet have. That is a good interpretation, but we can also look at it another way. Think about it like this. If all that was required was for us to discover the gifts we were given along with some training from our family, there would be no opportunity for us to create or add to our own life. Essentially we would add God's gifts to our family's contribution and that would be it, all we had. Though this may seem like enough for many, it lacks the element of our own input to our own life. This scripture tells us that we have a lot more power than we realize, though. We *can* do some seeking and not only find the gifts we already have but also acquire whatever it is that we need to enjoy the life we have and to create the relationships and lives that we want.

Many have heard the statement that the biggest gesture of agency we can have is to submit our will to God, and I agree, but what does this mean? At one level it means being willing to do whatever God asks when He asks, but what else could it suggest?

Maybe it also means submitting our will to Him. Meaning, He wants us to submit a plan (our will) of goodness, to Him so that He can help us to refine it and act on it. Maybe when He asks us to submit our will to Him, not only does He want us to be willing to follow His directions, but He also wants us to be anxiously engaged in creating plans of goodness that can also be submitted to Him for refinement and joint venturing.

As a father, I am often pleased when my children do just as I say. It is a moment of great joy to know they will listen and act according to my directions. It is also very pleasing when my children come to me with a plan of goodness that they have created on their own and ask for my help in refining it. This is a sublime moment for a parent as they see the creation of their offspring's heart, head, and hands and have the opportunity to support them. This is a moment of great closeness for parent and child as they share in creation, and the parent begins to see their offspring define their own life and grow through their choices and actions.

What do we want to add to our life? What do we want to create with our life? What do we want to become? When the Lord said to seek for the best gifts, He was saying, go creativity shopping, figure out what you want to add to your life, and try it. God wants us to create a life we can enjoy and share with Him and others.

The Ends of Creation

As we create, we have the opportunity to commune with deity and be filled with light and love as we work side by side with our Father in Heaven to bring hope to the world. Also, as we participate in the here and now creating our own healthy life, we experience the joy of being present with ourselves. Creating allows us to focus our energy in the now thus keeping our life current and vibrant. Additionally, many of our best memories are formed when we are engaged in creation: our family, our home, our relationships, our career, and our connection with God. Plus, when we are actively engaged in creating, we look forward to tomorrow, and we look fondly on the past as we see our creations. "And God saw everything that he had made, and, behold, it was very good" (Genesis 1:31).

Remember President Uchtdorf's counsel, "You may think you don't have talents, but that is a false assumption, for we all have talents and gifts, every one of us." The bounds of creativity extend far beyond the limits of a canvas or a sheet of paper and do not require a brush, a pen, or the keys of a piano. Creation means bringing into existence something that did not exist before—colorful gardens, harmonious homes, family memories, flowing laughter.

What you create doesn't have to be perfect. So what if the eggs are greasy or the toast is burned? Don't let fear of failure discourage you. Don't let the voice of critics paralyze you—whether that voice comes from the outside or the inside.

If you still feel incapable of creating, start small. "Try to see how many smiles you can create, write a letter of appreciation, learn a new skill, identify a space and beautify it."[5]

By choosing to seek the best gifts, we are creating a life that is in harmony with our Father in Heaven and also a life that He (Heavenly Father) can participate in with us. Through creating, we are renewed and connected to God; through creation, we are more present with ourselves in the now!

Notes

1. J. R. R. Tolkien, "On Fairy Stories," in Christopher Tolkien, ed., *Tree and Leaf: Including the Poem Mythopoeia* (New York: Houghton Mifflin, 1989), 50.
2. Dustin B. Thoman, Jessi L. Smith, and Paul J. Silvia, "The Resource Replenishment Function of Interest," Philosophy of the Social Sciences, March 28, 2011, accessed September 03, 2018, http://journals.sagepub.com/doi/abs/10.1177/1948550611402521.
3. Dieter F. Uchtdorf, "Happiness, Your Heritage," *Ensign*, November 2008, 118.
4. Marlin K. Jensen, "Living after the Manner of Happiness," *Ensign*, December 2002, 56–62.
5. Uchtdorf, "Happiness, Your Heritage."

Part Four

Walk with Christ

Jesus saith unto him, Rise, take up thy bed, ***and walk.***

—John 5:8

From time to time the question has been posed, "If Jesus appeared to you today, what questions would you ask of Him?"

My answer has always been, "I would not utter a word. I would listen to Him."

Down through the generations of time, the message from Jesus has been the same. To Peter by the shores of beautiful Galilee, He said, "Follow me.'" To Philip of old came the call, "Follow me." To Levi who sat at receipt of customs came the instruction, "Follow me." And to you and to me, if we but listen, shall come that same beckoning invitation, "Follow me."

—Thomas S. Monson

("Christ at Bethesda's Pool," *Ensign*, November 1996, 16.)

Conclusion

Your Atonement Is Now: Walk with Christ from the Pool of Bethesda

Dave was the saddest I'd seen him in a long time. Not a lot of anger was in him, but he was definitely sad. The divorce was now finalized, and his wife had majority custody. He got the kids every other weekend, rotating holidays, and for two weeks in the summer. The marital house was under contract. His wife was going back to work, and the kids were carrying on with life as if this was the way things had always been.

He could go to all the kids' school and sporting events, though, and he did. That way he could at least see them every week. But even that felt strange. In part because he had never really gone to those things before and partly because it was weird to see his wife (ex-*wife, he had to remind himself*) *and kids all there without him. It filled him with a sadness he didn't know how to cover.*

"I didn't realize it. All those times when I was at work putting in longer hours and all those nights when I was on the computer, I was losing out. I told myself it didn't matter because they were so little or because they were asleep. But it did matter. That's why the kids can move on with life and I can't. They're used to doing things without me."

This was a painful realization for Dave to come to. And there really wasn't anywhere for that pain to go, at least that he could see, so he just kept turning it back on himself.

"I'm such an idiot, James. I'm such an idiot. I can't believe I ever thought I could change this or make it up to Jennifer. Of course she divorced

me. Of course my kids don't like me. Look at who I am. I'm nothing. All I know how to do is work and hide stuff on the internet."

"Dave, you know that isn't true. You're still a child of God. You are still covered by Christ's Atonement. What about the goals we've been setting? What about getting to know yourself better and working through the Addiction Recovery Program? Don't you think you're making progress in those areas?" I tried to break through his distorted thoughts. "You're judging yourself so harshly now."

"Who cares if I am? I deserve it! Look at my life! I've lost everything."

There was an intensity to his emotions that was not usual for Dave. Something big was working its way out.

"Dave. Stop for just a minute. I understand how you feel. It's a normal part of the grieving process to get down on yourself and feel upset. But slow down for just a second and check your thoughts. Are your emotions telling you the truth? Is you being an idiot really the whole story?"

Dave put his head in his hands and didn't respond. Being upset was easy. Being honest with himself was not.

Words didn't seem to be getting through to him, so I started to draw a picture instead. On the left edge of the page I drew a large cloud bulging toward the middle of the page. I drew a second cloud on the right edge doing the same thing. In the middle I drew a stick figure with a bubble around him getting squished by the clouds.

I put the picture where Dave could see it. "Dave, do you know what these two clouds represent?"

He answered my question with a tired stare. I decided to give him a hint. I labeled the cloud on the left side of the page "the past" and I labeled the cloud on the right side of the page "the future."

"How are you feeling about your past and your future right now, Dave?"

"My past is just one long string of mistakes. And my future? I don't have one. I've lost everything."

I pointed to the stick figure in the middle. "So that's you. You're the guy whose past and future are making it impossible for him to do anything, right? It's game over. You're stuck forever in this middle space, this moment right now, with nothing but sadness and regret and worry. And there's no getting out of it."

Dave's stare glazed over as he succumbed to the fatigue that was cutting through his grief.

I let it sit for a minute, and then I drew another stick figure, but this one was above the clouds and, in his stick figure way, reaching down toward Dave.

When I spoke my voice was quiet. "Dave, there is a way out of it. We've been talking about Him for months. Are you ready to actually try living it?" Dave replied, "I think I'm ready."

Carolyn was pensive but not in her usual anxious manner. Instead of letting herself be dragged into some future worries, she was remembering her early married years and the woman she was then, who was a very different person from who she was now.

"If you saw me then, James, you wouldn't even recognize me. We were poor. I mean, poor. *Definitely did the paycheck-to-paycheck thing. Even after we both finished college and got good jobs. For whatever reason, we just couldn't get ahead of the student loans and the car payments. We were in a car accident that totaled the car, but the insurance didn't cover the cost of a new one, of course. My husband's back had been injured, and his face was torn up in the wreck. It wasn't life threatening, but it meant he couldn't go back to work for several months. Our oldest was not quite three, our second was about six months old, and we had just found out we were pregnant with baby number three . . . surprise! I thought we were stressed the day I took that pregnancy test, but after the wreck I was beyond stressed. I don't think there's even a word for what I was feeling then. Money was running out, and despite all my success in high school and college, there was nothing I could do to help my family.*

"Long story short, we ended up on bishops' storehouse. The shame was so thick I thought it would choke me. I worked hard all my life. I went to church. I paid my tithing. I had a temple recommend. I was married and having kids. But somehow it all fell apart and we were a wreck anyway.

"I was so scared and felt like dirt the first time I went to the storehouse. When the missionaries greeted me, I couldn't even look them in the eye. But they just kept talking and pushing my cart and playing with my kids and filling my bags with the food, and by the time we were done I just felt—I'm not sure, but it was a warm feeling—a loved feeling. It didn't matter that I had a college degree or that I used to be someone who could do everything alone. It didn't matter that I needed help now. All that mattered was that

I was there, and so they were going to love me. It was the closest to Christ I have ever felt. When I got in the car I thought that maybe for the first time I actually understood the Atonement. It was really as simple as a cart of groceries and a smile."

I still wasn't sure where she was going with this story so I prompted, "That's a beautiful story. Why are you telling me that today?"

"Because it occurred to me the other day that it has been years since I felt that kind of love, years since I felt that close to the Spirit. My oldest was crying over a report card—a long list of Bs—because it wasn't perfect. And seeing those tears . . . it hit me hard. I'm doing this wrong. I'm raising them wrong. I'm raising them to achieve, but I'm not raising them to love, to believe, to feel worthwhile. I'm doing this wrong."

"Not wrong, Carolyn. But maybe not with eternity in mind. When you were in the bishops' storehouse, you let go of a lot of pride and external value systems. You relied on the Lord and let Him determine your value. And that felt different, didn't it?" I questioned.

"Yes, but . . ."

"But what? Was the impression you had then wrong? Was that love you felt only meant to be there for a little while?" I pressed her. She was so close to seeing. I couldn't let the moment pass.

"No. That impression was real. It was the right feeling. But I don't feel it now. Maybe because I'm doing things wrong."

"Carolyn, were you doing things wrong when you needed help before?"

"No. We were stuck, and the only way to get out was to get help."

"So that love came because you needed help then. You need help now. Don't you believe you could feel that again? Feel it today, right now, every moment?"

Carolyn pursed her lips and looked far away for a moment. Then she replied, her voice quavering, "Yes. I would like to. But I don't know how."

I smiled and patted her hand. "The fact that you are able to say that means you are finally ready to learn how."

Lana started talking before she even made it all the way in the door.

"James, I did it."

She took a deep breath, and her face settled into a more serious expression. "I took the sacrament again."

I smiled. "Nice. How was it?"

"It was . . . I don't know. It wasn't what I expected."

"How do you mean? Did your ward switch to gluten-free bread or something?"

She laughed and rolled her eyes. "So, it's been a really long time since I took the sacrament. Like, more than a year. And at first I really felt bad about it. But then, as the months went by, I didn't feel bad anymore. It was just something that other people did but not me. Sometimes I'd watch the girls take it and then feel bad about it, but not other than that. But when the bishop told me it was time to start taking it again, I got scared." Lana stopped and took a few deep breaths, seemingly lost in thought.

"I remember you saying that you were scared because you were afraid you might mess up again, and the punishment would be worse. Is that what scared you?" I prompted.

"Well, yeah. But, like, I broke up with Jared for good. I deleted him from my phone and email. I blocked him on Facebook, Instagram, and Pinterest. We haven't had contact in months. And thinking about him and the choices I made, I don't know, I feel kind of sick. And sad. So sad for myself. Like, how could I let myself make decisions that were so clearly not *good for me? The bishop says that's how he knows my repentance is real. The sin isn't appealing to me anymore."*

Lana got lost in her own thoughts at that point. After gazing out the window for a minute she started again.

"And I guess that's true. I guess I have really repented, but I don't know. I still don't trust myself. Like, who's to say that I won't meet someone else and screw up again? My bishop says that he thinks I'll be fine, but I don't know. I'm gonna wait a while before I try dating again. Anyway, so when I could see the deacons coming with the sacrament tray I got super nervous. I started praying, and I just kept thinking, "Please, Lord, don't let me be a screwup. Please don't let me be a screwup. Am I really worthy? Can I really commit to do this?"

"If only everyone took it so seriously."

"That's what my bishop said too."

"What did you do when the bread came to you?"

"Well, I took it. Like, I just decided to take the sacrament and see. You know, like, if I screw up, I screw up. I don't want to, but as of Sunday I was fine, so why not take advantage of it? In that moment, I was completely

worthy to make those covenants. In that moment I was keeping them to the best of my ability, and, for just a moment, maybe, I was good enough. And if I could do it for one moment, I could probably do it the next and the next. When I thought that, my heart just lit up. Like, for a minute I could see my future, and it was bright and happy and what my girls need. It was great."

I don't often weep in the office, but hearing Lana talk, I teared up a bit. She finally got it. "Lana, you are definitely enough. What you felt is the power of the Atonement. It was happening in that moment, and it is still happening now. You can have that enough feeling every moment because of Jesus Christ."

Is It Waste or Is It Fertilizer?

One of the comments I hear most often in my office is usually something along these lines, "My life is such a mess! I made all these mistakes, and everything is just wrecked. What a waste!" Male or female, stay-at-home parent or working parent, teenager or adult, everyone at one point or another feels like the sum total of their choices is a complete and total pile of dung.

Now, that's a bit of a rough statement, but it's an extremely common feeling. So common, in fact, that I have a response at the ready. Whenever someone starts to tell me that all they have left is a pile of poop, I ask them one question: What's the difference between waste and fertilizer?

That question is often greeted with incredulous stares and silence.

I like to raise animals on my property. I always have llamas. I like to have a cow too. We've had dogs, chickens, and a few other critters from time to time. Regardless of the number of animals we have, one thing is constant: poop. All the animals do it, all the time. Depending on how many we have, we sometimes have a lot of piles of the smelly stuff all over their enclosures.

Now, when I see those piles I have a choice. I can see them as a complete waste, a giant mess to clean up, an unrelenting chore that makes for a bleak existence. Or, I can see those piles as an asset. I can see them as potentially useful. In fact, with some work and some time, those piles of stink can be turned into the perfect manure mix to fertilize my garden so it will flourish.

That's the challenge for every client who walks through my door: Will they take the crappier parts of their life, put in some work, give it some time, and use it as something to promote growth, or will they simply let it sit and stink up their lives?

Bethesda and Waste

One of the most amazing things about our Father in Heaven is His ability to work all things for our good. In Romans 8:28 we are told, "And we know that all things work together for good to them that love God, to them that are called according to his purpose." In the Doctrine and Covenants the Lord reassures the prophet Joseph Smith that even though he is in jail (again) and falsely accused of any number of things that he can take heart. "Peace be unto thy soul; thine adversity and thine afflictions shall be but a small moment; And then, if thou endure it well, God shall exalt thee on high" (121:7–8).

There are countless other examples throughout scripture of God taking someone's hard times and making it into something beautiful. Think about Moses and his sojourn in the wilderness. If he hadn't had that lonely trip through the desert on his own he would never have discovered God and been able to lead the Hebrews out of Egypt. Or, for an example on a smaller scale, think of Nephi and his bow. Nephi breaking his bow was a tragedy for their family, but it also turned into an opportunity for Nephi to get to know the Lord better and for God to show His love for Nephi.

Think of the man waiting at the pool of Bethesda. How many years was he there? How much time did he spend laying by that pool waiting to be healed? How many fixes did he try before going to the pool? All those years of waiting and trying and failing to be healed could have been thought of as a waste. None of it worked. None of it made his life easier. None of it got him what he wanted.

Or maybe it did.

Perhaps if he hadn't had those years of being sick and trying and failing, he wouldn't have been ready to hear the Lord's call when it came. Or maybe his suffering gave the people around him more opportunities to serve. It's unfathomable the number of reasons why this man's life of suffering happened, but it is obvious that with faith in Christ, nothing in his life went to waste.

It really all depends on how you look at it. Were those man's efforts a waste, or were they the tilling and fertilizing of the soil of his soul so that when the right season came he could experience unprecedented growth?

The Process of Preparing for Growth Happens Now

To successfully turn my animals' waste into useful manure for my garden, there are several necessary ingredients: waste, other organic material, water, sunshine, time, and work. Each of these has a unique, necessary role. If you skip any of them, the waste will either take longer to turn into useful fertilizer for the garden or it will not turn into anything useful at all.

Without preparation and some thoughtfulness, I'll end up with just a big pile of poop.

Our lives are the same way, especially when we hit on hard times. Our difficult marriages, our poor parenting decisions, the sins and weaknesses of the people around us, our own bad habits, our sins and weaknesses, our illnesses in all their varieties can be turned to good . . . but only if we properly prepare ourselves and apply some thoughtfulness. We have to be willing to do some work before we can turn our difficulties into prime areas of growth.

Instead of water, sunshine, and time, we need a few other things to compost our difficulties. First, we need humility to reach out to the Lord for help. Humility really is life-giving water for our souls. We need to be humble enough to remember that we are His *children* and we have to trust Him. We also need to take time to bask in the light of Christ's love; the Son of God was sent to help us all grow. This, of course, takes patience. Often, time has to pass in order for the Lord to work in our lives. We also have to be willing to do the daily work of turning our hearts to the Lord through prayer and scripture study. We have to be willing to remember that He loves us as only a perfect parent can and that He is constantly reaching out to us to teach us and help us. And we have to be willing to look at ourselves, our thought patterns, our practices, and our subconscious beliefs to see how they are holding us back from feeling God's love every minute of our lives.

Now, that sounds like a long list, but that is exactly what each of the attitudes and practices in this book are meant to do for you. Need help finding true humility? Turn down the voices in your head and stop lying to yourself. Want to bask in the light of the Son's love? Slow down and breathe. His love is evident in every breath we take, if we just take a moment to notice it. Do you want to develop patience to accept the Lord's timetable? Focus on creating the life you want, and the time that you spend waiting on the Lord will go by faster than you imagined.

The Joy of the Harvest

The best part of gardening is always the harvest. It's exciting to see the sprouts and buds and to watch the plants grow, but nothing beats the joy of the harvest. It never ceases to amaze me how a single cucumber seed can provide dozens of cucumbers, enough to feed my family and make pickles. Or a tiny carrot seed can produce an amazingly orange, tasty carrot bigger than my hand. Even if you've never gardened, you know the power of a single zucchini seed to feed an entire neighborhood.

In Galatians 6, we are reminded that "whatsoever a man soweth, that shall he also reap. For he that soweth to his flesh shall of the flesh reap corruption; but he that soweth to the Spirit shall of the Spirit reap life everlasting. And let us not be weary in well doing: for in due season we shall reap, if we faint not" (7–9).

Harvesting the fruits of our labors is a joyful part of the gardening process, and it is meant to be a joyful part of our lives. In my experience, if you have spent the time necessary to turn the piles of mistakes and frustrations and worries and errors and sins in your own life into life-giving spiritual compost, the harvest is full of not just happiness but also peace of mind, an easing of the conscience, and joy on an eternal scale. There is a resiliency that comes only from that kind of growth. The best part? When you start the spiritual harvest, reaping what you have sown in humility and faith and patience and repentance and love, Christ's Atonement provides life-giving water that produces a harvest every moment, not just every once in a while.

The harvest of living with the Atonement now hit home with me one night when one of my kids came to me and asked if we could go for a ride in the car. It was evening, and I got the feeling that my child might be struggling with something. As we got in the car, my child asked if he could ride in the back seat. A heavy feeling settled in my stomach. I felt this was going to be an evening of heartache.

As my child explained the struggles he was dealing with in his life, I was profoundly grateful for a realization I had come to just a couple of months earlier. One evening while sitting and reflecting on the Atonement of Christ, I realized that He had already forgiven me for everything I would do wrong tomorrow, and I didn't even know what that was going to be.

As this incredible thought soaked into my heart, I became aware of an opportunity I had never seen before. If Christ has already forgiven me for what I will do wrong tomorrow, then I too should forgive my fellow man for tomorrow's trespasses, even though I do not know what they will be.

This thought had an incredibly freeing power. I didn't have to wait to see what would happen and decide how hurt I am before I forgive. I can forgive today all that will happen tomorrow so that I can be free to love, serve, and be in the now. Our future can be free of worry because Christ has conquered it through His Atonement, and He has offered us that freedom if we will just have faith in Him.

As our two-hour car drive came to an end, my heartbroken child said five simple words to me, "Can you ever forgive me?" With love and tears, I was able to say, "I forgave you yesterday. How can I love and support you?" As our car pulled in the driveway, my child stated, "I think I should go see our bishop. Would you come with me?"

Just as it was for me as a young man visiting my bishop for the first time, shame and secrets had been avoided, honesty and love had been felt, hope and a chance to be whole again lay ahead. Christ's Atonement was working for both my son and me in the now.

Remembering the Lessons of Bethesda

That is the real lesson of Bethesda, that Christ comes into our lives not just to provide relief from pain but also to heal us in our entirety. He performed the Atonement, He suffered in Gethsemane for our sins and worries and fears and stresses and anxieties, precisely because He wanted to be able to heal us. He never meant to provide only an aspirin for the roughest moments of our lives. Every step He took, every word He uttered, every pain He felt, and every drop of His blood that was spilled was for our complete and total healing. He spent every moment of His life preparing to heal us in every moment of our lives, if we will let Him, if we will follow Him. It is exactly as He told us, "For behold, I, God, have suffered these things for all, that they might not suffer if they would repent" (Doctrine and Covenants 19:16).

The primary ingredients to prepare ourselves for growth are laid out in the previous chapters of this book, and it is my hope that you'll return to the book often to be reminded of God's love for you right now and how to better access that love. But if there is only one thing you remember, I hope you will remember that Heavenly Father's love is real, and it is happening right *now*. Christ's promise of healing is real, and it is happening right *now*. The Atonement is real, and it is happening *now*.

So, rise, take up your bed, and start your walk with Christ right now and be made whole.

Bibliography

Cohen, Elizabeth. "Does Life Online Give You 'popcorn Brain'?" CNN. June 23, 2011. Accessed September 03, 2018. http://www.cnn.com/2011/HEALTH/06/23/tech.popcorn.brain.ep/index.html?eref=rss_health&utm_source=feedburner&utm_medium=feed&utm_campaign=Feed: rss/cnn_health (RSS: Health).

Cuda, Gretchen. "Just Breathe: Body Has A Built-In Stress Reliever." NPR. December 06, 2010. Accessed September 03, 2018. http://www.npr.org/2010/12/06/131734718/just-breathe-body-has-a-built-in-stress-reliever.

Flint, Alan J., Ashley N. Gearhardt, William R. Corbin, Kelly D. Brownell, Alison E. Field, and Eric B. Rimm. "Food-addiction Scale Measurement in 2 Cohorts of Middle-aged and Older Women | The American Journal of Clinical Nutrition | Oxford Academic." OUP Academic. January 22, 2014. Accessed September 03, 2018. http://ajcn.nutrition.org/content/early/2014/01/22/ajcn.113.068965.short.

Harvard Health Publishing. "Why Stress Causes People to Overeat." Harvard Health Blog. July 18, 2018. Accessed September 03, 2018. http://www.health.harvard.edu/newsletter_article/why-stress-causes-people-to-overeat.

"How Many People Are on Porn Sites Right Now? (Hint: It's a Lot.)." Fight the New Drug. April 02, 2018. Accessed September 03, 2018. http://fightthenewdrug.org/by-the-numbers-see-how-many-people-are-watching-porn-today/.

Kleinman, Alexis. "Porn Sites Get More Visitors than Netflix, Amazon and Twitter Combined." The Huffington Post. December 07, 2017.

Accessed September 03, 2018. https://www.huffingtonpost.com/2013/05/03/internet-porn-stats_n_3187682.html.

Ophir, Eyal, Clifford Nass, and Anthony D. Wagner. "Cognitive Control in Media Multitaskers." Google Scholar. September 15, 2009. Accessed September 03, 2018. https://scholar.google.com/citations?view_op=view_citation&hl=en&user=2trZ2IYAAAAJ&citation_for_view=2trZ2IYAAAAJ:UebtZRa9Y70C.

Partnership News Service. "New Data Show Millions of Americans with Alcohol and Drug Addiction Could Benefit from Health Care Reform - Where Families Find Answers on Substance Use | Partnership for Drug-Free Kids." Partnership for Drug-Free Kids - Where Families Find Answers. September 28, 2010. Accessed September 03, 2018. https://drugfree.org/learn/drug-and-alcohol-news/new-data-show-millions-of-americans-with-alcohol-and-drug-addiction-could-benefit-from-health-care-reform.

Pedram, Pardis, Danny Wadden, Peyvand Amini, Wayne Gulliver, Edward Randell, Farrell Cahill, Sudesh Vasdev, Alan Goodridge, Jacqueline C. Carter, Guangju Zhai, Yunqi Ji, and Guang Sun. "Food Addiction: Its Prevalence and Significant Association with Obesity in the General Population." PLOS Medicine. September 4, 2013. Accessed September 03, 2018. http://journals.plos.org/plosone/article?id=10.1371/journal.pone.0074832.

Sederer, Lloyd. "A Blind Eye to Addiction." U.S. News & World Report. June 1, 2015. Accessed September 03, 2018. http://www.usnews.com/opinion/blogs/policy-dose/2015/06/01/america-is-neglecting-its-addiction-problem.

"Sexual Addiction and Compulsivity Research Bibliography." SASH. 2017. Accessed September 03, 2018. http://www.sash.net/sexual-addiction-and-compulsivity-research-bibliography/.

Szalavitz, Maia. "How Orphanages Kill Babies—and Why No Child under 5 Should Be in One." The Huffington Post. November 17, 2011. Accessed September 03, 2018. http://www.huffingtonpost.com/maia-szalavitz/how-orphanages-kill-babie_b_549608.html.

Thoman, Dustin B., Jessi L. Smith, and Paul J. Silvia. "The Resource Replenishment Function of Interest." Philosophy of the Social Sciences. March 28, 2011. Accessed September 03, 2018. http://journals.sagepub.com/doi/abs/10.1177/1948550611402521.

Tovian, Steve, PhD, Beverly Thorn, PhD, Helen Coons, PhD, Susan LaBott, PhD, Matthew Burg, PhD, Richard Surwit, PhD, and Daniel Bruns, PhD. "Stress Effects on the Body." Monitor on Psychology. Accessed September 03, 2018. http://www.apa.org/helpcenter/stress-body.aspx.

Ward, Mark. "Web Porn: Just How Much Is There?" BBC News. July 01, 2013. Accessed September 03, 2018. https://www.bbc.com/news/technology-23030090.

Willcox, Bradley J., D. Craig. Willcox, and Makoto Suzuki. *The Okinawa Program: How the Worlds Longest-Lived People Achieve Everlasting Health—and How You Can Too.* New York: Three Rivers Press, 2002.

Acknowledgments

I once listened to a man eulogizing his wife. He said something about her that has stuck with me for years and still carries significant weight. The man said, "I was married to a woman who believed in me; how could I ask for more?"

I am grateful to my wife for believing in me, even though at times that belief is probably not justified. Her inspiration and love compels me to be a better man, and it has also made so many things that are impossible possible.

I am also thankful to my mother and how she taught me to think freely and broadly. She is a woman filled with ideas and views. She would often invent titles to new books that she planned on writing one day. Often her titles would capture the essence of her book even though a book was never written. In many ways, this is the book she never wrote but inspired me to write.

To my children, thank you for being you. I have often said to my kids, "When I grow up, I want to be like you." That is still true today.

To my brothers and sister, thank you for your openness, your kindness, and your love. This book is a witness to the loving relationship I have had with you my entire life.

To my friends, I am amazed at the quality of people I have had the privilege of associating with throughout my life. Your influence is also felt in the pages of this book. Thank you!

And finally to my Father in Heaven, my Savior Jesus Christ, and the Holy Spirit—I am grateful for Thy grace, inspiration, and hope. Thankfully, I am forever in Your debt.

About the Author

If you asked James Skeen what his long-term goal is, he would tell you it is the reconciliation of the family of man. James has degrees in economics and marketing and a master's in behavioral science counseling. He is a licensed professional counselor and has served as a bishop and a seminary teacher for many years. For James, the concept of *I Forgave You Yesterday* became reality while hiking and camping alone in the Rocky Mountains of Colorado in the summer of 2010. It may have been the clear air, the night sky, or the smell of earth that helped him see the human struggle more clearly than he had ever seen it before, but as James drove home from his wilderness experience, he knew that Christ's Atonement was more than just a reaction to sin—it was the way to being present in life again and becoming whole now. James has been married to his wife, Brenda, for thirty-three years. They have three kids and live in Loveland, Colorado. He still loves to hike in the Rocky Mountains with his llamas and is grateful for the blessing of family, friends, and the gospel every day.

Scan to visit

www.jamesskeen.com